Chess Parenting

Fritz Blackburn

Chess Parenting

Fritz Blackburn

Cover design: Bernhard Riegler
    Photo: Fritz Blackburn
    Book design: Fritz Blackburn
    Editor: Jessica Montegrejo

Online copy provided in New Zealand
Published by Fritz Blackburn
mailto: Readblackburn@gmail.com

Contents – Index

Chapter 1: Responsibility and Self-discipline

"I hate school" screams my fifteen-year old female descendant. "They always tell you what to do and it's all gay old bull anyway." I can't honestly disagree, having hosted similar feelings towards an institution that forced uninteresting information on me that I could not question and that treated me with absolute authority rather than with respect.

I like learning things only after verifying them for myself. My kids are like that too.

Surely, it is better for kids to have opportunity and time to develop character, emotional experience and mind mastery, than it is to have second hand knowledge shovelled down their throats? The school curriculum is much more concerned with producing workers for existing machines, with yesterday's economic and political utilities and with social engineering, than it is with reaching for the human potential.

In our day, family and village no longer foster social ability or offer anything like rites of passage or any actual initiation into adulthood! Schools are supposed to take on such functions but don't.

"Sit down then. Let's play a game of chess!" "Yeaah! I'll whip your ass, dad," wails a pleased monster teenager...

We've been doing this ever since the girls could hold a pawn without eating it, and I do like the results. They're not as nuts now from their overdosing on oestrogen as they otherwise would be...

To experience that you can win against an adult, this species who always "knows best" and is "always right," when you're seven—that changes *everything*! Authority no longer comes automatically with age but wants to be earned, which means a kid can have the authority! Why should a smart kid listen to grown-ups who obviously can't think very clearly...? But an adult who masters his own mind—he really deserves the respect others may demand only because of their age!

Here is the chance for a kid to "overcome her parent"—so she does not need to engage in more serious hostilities later...here a boy can safely "murder" his father and so resolve his Oedipus-grudge without hurting him! Here a girl can show her equal (or superior...) female logic!

The resulting equal footing and respect in the parent/teenager relationship is worth a million dollars! It is the basis for true, joyful learning and self-development, without any need for demands, control, punishments or force!

The girls whipped nearly every adult player in the Bay of Islands by age twelve and were possessed by a deep sense of self-respect and self-reliance. It translated into all the other walks of life they tried. They won all their karate tournaments, decorating our home with trophies and medals, and they made blackbelt at ages twelve and fifteen, the little one winning gold at the New Zealand Nationals at age eleven. She also played key-board, her sister the guitar and flute, and both made plenty of other successful and happy noises throughout their childhood.

But to have them go quiet as church mice, chess would be the solo-dad's best weapon! No fighting, no boredom, no "hanging."

And, quite playfully, it pushes for excellence...

Most people understand that chess helps mathematical skills and logic. But it is so much more than that! Here we have a tool to bring out those quintessential human skills or values, that are so neglected and ignored today, like self-discipline, self-respect, responsibility, good judgement, creative visualization and truth-seeking!

Kids love to play, as do all sane adults. Learning works much better inside a game of skill. Today, children don't play enough, and never unsupervised, and never responsible unto themselves, which stifles brain development considerably. Playtime is not respected as such by parents and increasingly sacrificed for structured agendas. With chess, you have both!

However—what they learn here is not graciously handed down arbitrary, second-hand knowledge, but instead the ability to use their own minds, to reason and see what *is* and to act on their own fresh ideas. School fosters storing archival knowledge, but chess fosters intelligence and the discernment between truth and illusion!

On the surface, chess appears to be more mental than physical or emotional. To play chess well, however, one needs to be physically fit (oxygenated), and learn to let go of tensions from useless emotions like wanting to win, fearing to lose, anger at mistakes, doubt, or feeling pressured! To free the mind of distractions and negative attitudes plays a major part in emotional intelligence and in cleansing the mind from clutter and background noise. Only where the mind is clear can we have deeper insights and authentic feelings.

Emotions are mental by-products of a struggling mind. Jealousy and anger are obvious examples. Only when the mind is at ease, unburdened by troublesome emotions and imaginations, can we become truly capable to engage in friendship, real love, in un-avoided sadness, accepting grief and fearless happiness, and all other real feelings...

Chess is even more effective at this shedding of false emotions than hugging!

Chess presents as formidable a Zen-discipline as do archery, tea-ceremony or the arranging of flowers. The Japanese are quite innocent of chess however; the kingly game came from the Persian/ Chinese cultural circles, where it manifests the principles of yin and yang and of Taoist harmony.

Chess is a duality game, where black and white respond to each other in describing a universe of polar opposites that is uncannily symbolic of all reality. There is no limit to the depth of this interaction. You can never hope to learn all there is to know, or always win. You never stop learning the game for as long as you live! It remains forever fascinating, unmastered and new—a tool never to lose its mind-sculpting edge.

The best thing is—kids can win against adults, who lose their hiding place behind the number of their age or income...

Kids can prove their worth without ridicule here, which for boys is the second greatest need. There is then no fear of authoritative rulings or patronising paternal bull. Children can find actual truth underneath mere opinions, and real respect, which is what girls and boys need the most.

Can you imagine what it does for abstract thinking? We once played with river stones in a dried-out river bed, having no chess set...after a few hours we had become so used to the stones on the sandy landscape that we quite forgot about the lack of a proper set, and quite enjoyed a few pretty little games... You look at a rock and see a rook and a taller rock is the queen and eventually players learn to visualize enough to play "blind," which is entirely without board or pieces. This abstract visualization ability is what then marks the great scientist, researcher, CEO or artist...

And it teaches great discipline quite naturally and from within, instead of a "discipline" imposed against resistance, by a pestering and forever unsuccessful parent!

In matters of spiritual growth, which has nothing to do with religious concepts, our modern societies are poor and helpless. Who is teaching our kids to seek truth or to take responsibility for their own minds? Nobody even believes in truth as a value any more, sacrificing it with every step to opinion, to political correctness, and to convenience.

In chess, there is usually only one best or true move, beyond the hundred opinions!

To dig up that deeper truth, beyond views and appearances—that is the Tao of chess and the fast track to evolving mind and consciousness!

This pursuit of the true next move inevitably leads us on a journey, where we also meet those other values, like justice, courage, beauty. From there, it all just happens...

Not all kids like chess, of course. Lack of curiosity or of confidence is usually the reason. Those kids may profit from it even more...

There cannot really be an absence of interest in chess, where there is an interest in mind and in reaching for boundary...

There is however something about chess that many people thoroughly dislike: it forces us into being responsible! No dice, no chance, no blaming on anything else—we are solely responsible for the outcome, for the future of the game, for what we do now! We live with the consequences of our actions! And this is what makes chess such a formidable educational and spiritual tool!

Few things today are less recognised than the dreadful absence of consequences in modern children's lives! Proportionally to our own latent fears, we protect our kids from life, from painful experience and from the consequences of their actions or inactions until they are adults or at an age where they are supposed to be.

It starts with "don't touch that candle!" in an ominous and warning mother's voice, when a toddler slowly approaches the flame with her hand and it continues as a general and abrupt "don't touch!" for years. It continues every time we "rescue" our sweetie from real life, until they withdraw their hands and fail trying to "compre-hand" altogether...

We save them from bullies, from fever, from boredom, pain and work—and think it love when we clean up after them...

Here is the real reason for our rising crime rates and non-functional democracies—you can't get responsible adults by pampering kids into non-responsibility!!

It is only on top of this, that we save them from our own boredom by showing them violent films that put picture and proposal to those non-responsible, but wide-open minds, while we could at any time choose to become responsible ourselves and offer them some constructive educational alternatives…

Mind you—the ecological destruction of our planet is also mainly caused by non-responsible adults and only secondarily by chemicals. Not by children!

We don't really feel responsible for our own kids' education, which we leave to underfunded schools where bullies rule from top to bottom!

We feel not even responsible for our own health and leave the responsibility to doctors who make money from selling pills, plastic body-parts and antibiotics…

We are never responsible when our relationships fail, as we can blame our partners thereafter called "the bitch" and "the asshole."

We have built our societies in a way where the individual does not feel responsible. He may be "held" responsible, but he does not feel the courage of being responsible, nor the freedom or the beauty of it.

Unlike a king, who is responsible all his life, the prime minister and president today can order hundreds of thousands killed in illegal wars, without any reason, and then retire on a fat pension! He does not feel responsible for the deaths of innocents. Nor do any of us.

No peasants with pitchforks waiting outside the castle in democracies…

How can we expect our children to feel self-responsible?

When we travel to Kampuchea, seeing a seven-year old boy proudly running his own "business," networking with travellers or selling coconuts for six hours a day—we call that "child labour" and pity the little entrepreneur who can calculate, wears Adidas, and speaks English…

Schools talk lots of responsibilities and of consequences, and "teach" it as equating punishment. So, children dislike those two words, probably for good.

A fight in the school yard teaches much better about consequences ...and that is why it happens! The bully threatening to beat you into a pulp is actually teaching you more about taking care of yourself and about being responsible for yourself than the "rescuing" teacher or parent! This may be hard for a solo-dad of two girls to embrace—but it is the observable truth.

Let us be a little more controversial: If you never let a kid use a knife, because she could cut herself—you're causing your kid to become incompetent, insecure, anxious, dangerous and distrusted, with no faith in Self and with lowered intelligence! She cannot develop self-discipline, appropriate caution or confidence if she is not allowed to cut herself! Blood and pain are great teachers and deemed necessary by the natural world...This natural feedback for careless, casual or arrogant approaches cannot always be replaced with words!

In chess, children enter a world where they *always* face the consequences for what they do and see incorrectly, and where the future of any game is the fair outcome of their actions, insights, or lack thereof! Everything is fair, nothing left to happenstance.

They are totally and solely responsible here!

From this sense of being in charge grows true self-discipline, while imposed discipline can never possibly lead to that fine result. It creates only resistance and refusal and rejection of all teaching.

The lack of motivation in modern school kids comes from not being under their own steam! They want to be in charge and get hurt some!

Boot-camp in the jungle is great, but today unwieldy for most. Chess can be the answer for many here!

Chess players don't blame each other when they lose! They own their defeat. They look where they made the key mistake. This approach is what makes people successful at life in general! Mistakes in chess always become manifest and observable. They are not and cannot be hidden.

Two rules in chess that beginners learn first determine that once a piece is touched, it must be moved, and that moves once executed cannot be taken back. It is an act of discipline not to touch a piece while considering it! To touch a piece is like signing a contract—you are then committed to the move. That makes a player acutely aware of his responsibility to the game and to everything his acting hand does, here and now.

Once the queen is moved you cannot undo the move when you belatedly notice your queen will be lost. You must live with the consequences of an act already completed, which is of enormous psychological benefit. Rule of the jungle! No glass houses...

When you collect wet wood—you won't have fire! Once the oceans are destroyed, there is no way back...it's over! No move can ever be taken back...

The creation of a beautiful game or of a strong position has taken commitment and we feel a responsibility to ourselves to now bring it to a strong ending as well. It is a need to live up to ourselves and to persevere that arises not from some moral "Über-ich" or from a quest for parental praise, but from inside their own character—and gives birth to true self-discipline!

When you made a "silly" mistake and feel like giving up on a game—you cannot just wipe the pieces off the board! You have responsibilities to your partner also, who might like to continue playing it out. You learn respect and discipline from that too.

As it happens, these are all qualities in need of development if somebody intends to walk the spiritual path or just master life, or simply grow up. Especially responsibility! Followers of religions or other concepts never really enter this path. You cannot simultaneously be a follower and be self-responsible!

In order to become fully responsible, we need to deprogram our mind from cultural, religious and parental parameters and become free from automation. To be a freethinker is an absolute requirement for success in spiritual and creative endeavours.

Just like being a healer is a necessity when being a father... Leaving it all to doctors and antibiotics is not the path of a responsible father!

We need to expect the real solutions not from others, but from ourselves! Otherwise we are followers and copy-cats, not explorers responsible for their own destiny. To parents, responsibility must mean a focus on cultivating the already existing, undivided potential in their child, rather than to continue the repetitions of yesterday by means of imposing their own errors, divisions and illusions.

When it is your move, no book or grandmaster can advise you. There is no guru! You are alone. Alone with the responsibility to manifest yourself in your next move! Deciding what is true and what is illusion.

That is the beginning of chess-parenting.

Chapter 2: Truth and Illusion

"That's just an opinion!" "Let's agree to disagree!" "There is no absolute Truth!" These are the exclamations of our politically correct, democratic hearts…

It is an attitude where we no longer seek to find out what really is true for ourselves and where we trust the majority to do it for us. If we are Americans we may define all those who oppose us and Israel as terrorists. The Arabs naturally see those who bomb their families as the terrorists. Both groups are quite blind to any objective truth and see each other as evil and themselves as innocent fighters for freedom…

So, what is the absolute truth here? Do we even really want to know? The truth is that both parties see reality only from their own, divided, perspective, not as it actually is, since they are too busy deluding themselves by creating the spin centred on maintaining their divided views.

The obvious but unseen truth is that the killing of "terrorists" always creates new grievances and ever more terrorists… Truth is—we are not addressing the problem at all, nor do we believe in non-violent approaches any more than those others we call the terrorists. We utterly avoid the truth of this "unsolvable problem" because we do not wish to confront it or reveal our own fears and our own selfish, divided and militant motives. Nor do we wish to discover just to what extent weapon- and oil-companies are running our democracies and influence what we individually hold as true.

We never carry any debate to the inevitable underlying truths, but make it into a party-political issue every time, replacing truth with opinionated spin! We naturally do this in science as well, in religion—and in our relationships too, as all areas of life are ruled by the same attitudes and limited by our same limitations. We do it to our children every day!

There is of course no "objective" truth to topics like abortion or whether it is okay to help people die, but things in themselves are either true or not.

Does God exist? Does life have a purpose we might miss? Are we ourselves the actual terrorists who use violence even against our children and our animals?

Nobody asks such questions for fear of the truth. It isn't democratic to question the established majority view to such an uncomfortable point...Too painful!

Others decide for us what a terrorist is! Or rather—we buy their definitions without them ever even giving any...Political correctness is what we use to cover up uncomfortable truth, and "professionalism" is to go quiet or evasive when confronted with undesired truths.

What is the truth about global warming? That climate change is man-made? How self-important is that? And a dead miss of target! It gets warmer and colder independent of humans. It always has. We can only adapt to it, but not slow it or keep it stable. Climate change is real and a threat we need to face, but carbon credits won't do that! We are missing the truth!

Our *real* issues are with survival! The eradication of the last rainforests, the pollution of our oceans, water, soil and our own bodies are not mere threats in a possible future. Neither are earth-quakes and tsunamis! They are happening right now!

Yet nobody with powers to do so seriously thinks to stop the daily logging in the Amazon and Indonesia, or the ships spilling oil into the seas. We avoid the truth that we had to stop yesterday—to stop thinking as we do! We instead fool ourselves by having expensive, unserious meetings over global warming.

If somebody dares speaking real truth as in "Wiki-leaks," we soon call him a traitor and wish to execute him...

When a recession hits, we are asked to increase consumer spending! To "stimulate" what we call the economy! This is how we are. This is the truth about us.

We fool ourselves most if not all the time! We fear truth as the certain death of our lovely opinions!

And opinion is all we have today...all we can possibly pass on to our children.

"Majority opinion" has replaced actual truth and the personal responsibility of finding it!

The resulting complacency and hypocrisy have undermined all emotional honesty in the individual to the point of disorientation. Truth has become the most socially unacceptable topic, before death, incest and sex with animals...

So, given our own contempt for truth, our double-standards and hypocrisies—what on Earth makes parents think they should *expect* their kids to be truthful with them or to even respect them as honourable people?? Kids can easily see, sooner and later, that their parents are hypocrites, that they say one thing and act the opposite. And when they speak it out, we call them "disrespectful." No, we are not ready to teach about truth by a long shot! A responsible parent realizes that and works on himself first and foremost in that regard! A kid only becomes an "honest" person where a parent or other person consistently shows them how that is done! Therefor *always* be truthful with yourself and with your kid, starting as a baby, without exceptions! Truth can be spoken on any subject to any age in the appropriate way—or should be!

I have never once lied to any of my kids and never felt tempted. I know that works.

But even a kid raised to be truth-loving usually cannot keep it up in a truth-hostile environment! It has become too unfashionable to be authentic...

Angry employees are smiling warmly at their bosses, delinquent company directors at wary stockholders, priests at a blindly faithful congregation, the Pope at the "child-loving" cardinal, and the cheating wife at the trusting husband...

It is "normal" to tell kids about "Santa" and other stories known to be untrue. So they may get used to it early...

At school, the "truth" is only what authority demands they accept and copy, not something for kids themselves to discover!

At this stage, they usually give up on demanding or seeking truth...

We adults have long given up finding out our own innermost realities, since we do not feel responsible for that any longer! It is up to the philosophers, priests, doctors and scientists...

There are no absolute truths any more. Everything is relative. It is for extremists and fundamentalists only, to speak of absolute truth.

But fact is—there either *is* a God, or there is not, right? That is logic! We just usually don't know, but there *is* this absolute truth out there, quite apart from all perception...There either is—or is not a God, just like there either is or is not an elephant.

The universe either has a purpose or it is completely random! There is an absolute truth to that as well.

There either *is* an afterlife or there is not. An absolute truth with nothing in between! Our opinions about it are worthless as opinions usually are. Only the actual truth is of any use—if it can be detected!

The good news here is that truth isn't hidden! God doesn't hide and neither does truth...

It isn't impossible, or even difficult, to make out the truth. It just often can't be verified by those not yet ready to become conscious of it. There are certain steps to take first.

Truth cannot be passed on via words. It occurs only in a courageous mind free of illusion or ready to let go of illusion. In that sense, it remains always personal or subjective.

All practical spiritual effort is of course centred on the recognition of illusion as just that and the consequent recognition of deeper Truth. But how, short of meditating in caves and having near death experiences, can we get there today?

Given to us by nature, the experiences of being with dying people, with a divine lover, with women giving birth, or with your child—is what reveals to us the basic truths that anchor us to reality! Adults and children grounded in such experiences know real life and will not be easily fooled by appearances...

But here again—our culture prevents those main sources of insight from meeting the light of day! We mostly grow into "maturity" without having ever seen death or birth or people making love! And when we reach ages eighteen or twenty-one, we are declared adults as if the passing of time itself endowed people with wisdom, maturity or insight...

We therefore experience a breakdown of spiritual, social and emotional maturing in young people as we have never before...and also a deterioration of language that reflects our aversion against naming truth and enforces it.

Young females seem to dislike certain words and make up new ones. A belly becomes thus the "stomach" you "cannot even see any more," if you're with Jenny Craig, and the tearing out of vaginal hair is called "bikini waxing" even though no wax ever goes on any bikini. Calling it what it really is would likely make some girls think twice. So, they don't.

The extreme immaturity caused by this firm reluctance to face reality is not addressed at school or in correctional facilities or even in pregnancy or during illness, band often stays with us throughout adulthood! What is usually seen as "phases" by non-responsible parents, later becomes personal and then cultural identity and limitation.

But what can a young person do, if she wishes to discern between illusion and reality and feels ready to learn seeing things for what they really are?

Try playing chess! In chess, we also start out with opinions about a position and there are the same appearances hiding deeper truths. The great difference however is that the truth can easily be discovered and proven here, opinions refuted and appearances unmasked!

The truth prevails and cannot be escaped in chess! Sure, beginners still argue about the correct move and the better position, but the better players become, the more they all agree on those details.

Masters generally agree on these matters, simply because they have a consciousness that isn't fooled by illusion and thus can zoom in on objective reality.

Out of a thousand moves, Bobby Fisher would make (at least!) 999 times the same move God would! He approximates absolute truth and describes the world (a position) *as it is.* People never considered that at all, when he made political and philosophical remarks.

Ultimately, the longer a game goes on, the more it is about absolute, objective truth.

While in the opening the player has a wide choice of equivalent possibilities or relative truths, he finds towards the end stages that there is say a five-move forced checkmate. At this stage, chess is about finding this absolute truth which completes the game. That is the mastery of that position; it can be discovered and all illusions and opinions that disagree with that are easily proven false! Not by majority decision of course, but by the greatest present consciousness and by the absolute verifiability of chess.

Illusions naturally die in the facing of manifest truth. No rhetorical arguments help.

No agreeing to disagree, no "equal opinions!" Only the truth! It is possibly the most magnificent thing about the game of kings that it does not bow to the democratic demand of ignoring truth for majority-votes on reality!

Let us be sure to realize here that truth cannot be gathered or discerned by knowledge!

The seven-year old can find a more valid truth than his seventy-year old experienced opponent!

It is outlook and attitude, rather than knowledge that leads to the true move, in game and in life...

Truth is not something to figure out or think up. It rather occurs when we are responsible, sincere, relaxed, observing, don't jump to hasty judgements, and look from all available perspectives.

The vision of what is true is enabled by the eye of the beholder, not by any supposed objectivity, and that is why we must practise to look and see correctly by developing those values that allow us to achieve the necessary clarity.

Absolute truths have disappeared completely from our menu; we don't even believe in their existence now. Even in the natural sciences, everything is relative and opinion-based. It is far more important to agree with the professor's opinion or theory than to commit to our own research, and more important to make a profit than to do the right thing.

The truth is the unwanted and abandoned child we floated down the river...

There is one group of people we very rarely see in chess clubs—females! If we do the politically incorrect thing and ask after the actual reason for this, we must dig deeper than to shrug and state that chess is just not a female thing.

When girls are little, their brain and interest absolutely enable them to learn chess as well as boys do. But as soon as oestrogen seriously starts kicking in at around age fourteen, they usually lose their interest and the ability. One could think that oestrogen, which is known to shrink the brain, is the sole reason for this, or deny the phenomenon entirely. At the bottom of the observation, however, we find an inner cause:

Girls, lacking any form of initiation into womanhood in our society, manifest a severe lack of self-worth, self-responsibility, self-acceptance and realness at that age! Everything is then about appearance and nothing about reality or truth!

It is impossible to be overly concerned about appearance and to be a good chess player as well! Impossible, to wear make-up every day and be committed to authenticity at the same time! Or to even get interested in chess...

The trick is to develop the minds of girls when they are young, so they have some mental structure to fall back on later, when the hormonal disorientation begins.

Another group that has a hard time learning chess well are people who want to be "normal!" In New Zealand, this seems to be most people's dearest desire...

Recently, the winner of $ 36 million at lotto was asked what she would now do to change her life. She answered: "all I really want is to stay normal. We are normal people and just want to go on as normal!"

To be an "average kiwi," to be "normal" and an "ordinary bloke," to quote the major identity-forming imprints, is to be somebody *else*, that doesn't really exist. Like the famous English understatement, it is an ego-based fishing expedition for complements and acceptance while denying truth as it presents. Wanting to be "normal" is seeking identification with public opinion, and it betrays fear of personal truth. It makes self-development appear as weird and chess as a waste of time...

The least "normal" thing of all is of course—speaking the truth! It is weird, strange, outrageous, unbelievable and offensive to speak truthfully in public or in private.

It is even dangerous in our "free" societies, as Julian Assange is about to find out...It is no longer pc to speak the truth! Try and say in Germany or the US that Israel is the most militant, uncompromising and violent country, and not the poor, innocent victim or the "chosen people of God" it so excels in portraying itself as...

This is exceedingly true, but utterly "incorrect" and "offensive" to even mention in the English-and German-spoken world! And that is why only a few truth-committed people like Bobby Fisher or John Pilger dare say it...

In chess, speaking the perceived truth is always okay! It is in the very nature of the game to drop illusions and to manifest, act and speak the truth without censuring it!

Not only does absolute truth obviously exist, but it can be expressed without facing the usual social repercussions and diplomatic disasters! Truth wins out against illusion all of the time! Illusions and prejudice die painless deaths on every chess board, in every game...

Imagine you face a three-move forced mate. Most people can't see this and have wild opinions on how to continue. What they see is a bunch of illusions, followed by the conclusion that nothing is there to see or do. Out of hundred masters however, all one hundred would completely agree on how exactly it *is* done!

Those who disagree may have a democratic right to do so and even, as usual, be the majority, and they may loudly express their "equal" opinions, but nobody competent listens to them when they fail to show the truth of it!

Chess makes parents honest and competent and real!

A child who regularly discovers such objective truths like solutions to forced mates, stops caring for mere opinion and firmly sets his eye on the underlying reality behind appearances in general. He seeks the view that considers all...which is to take responsibility for what happens!

The great educational appeal in chess is the scope of its objective truths and their accessibility. Truth however, in a spiritual and everyday sense, is something very personal and subjective, as well as objective.

To face personal truth is a common experience in chess, and the feedback we constantly receive is like a mirror...

Bullies will always attack with powerful pieces, with no sense for defence. The fearful wall themselves into cramped fortifications and never come out. Beginners usually play only with one or two pieces, never connecting them up with all their other assets. Or they have a preference for white (if they are Christians), or a fear of losing the queen (if they are business-men), or they always make the same "silly" mistake because they cannot really commit.

Many make a move first and then look what happens...

All these patterns in chess- playing directly reflect the same active pattern in all other areas of this player's personal and emotional life and can be observed here without the usual filters, in I-Ging-like symbolism!

The guy who walls himself in, always loses through suffocation—which his partners, as well as the game itself, point out to him every time he does it. The guy, who attacks with two pieces, gets beaten until he uses three, four, and then all of his resources...and he would continue to get beaten in all other areas, all of his life, unless this is recognized and corrected early.

Wrong philosophies like isolationism, aggressive expansion or arrogance, quite simply don't work in chess and get eliminated. Manipulators have no hope—nothing can be manipulated. (Good players remember where all the pieces were, when they return from the bathroom...)

Those players, who play only to win and to dominate, find themselves unsuccessful and unhappy half the time, while those afraid of making a mistake will sit and think beyond their time without finding any concentration or joy.

If you are an impatient player or lack endurance—the other players will drag you into long, difficult end-games and thus give you the exact training and pain you most require—just as life is likely to do.

Anybody who observes this going on during a game will quite easily attain self-knowledge and can use chess as a mirror to see himself much clearer than in other situations. Our repetitive mistakes quickly become obvious as a discernible pattern. Soon we know whether we are too aggressive or too cautious, fearful or relaxed, isolated or well-connected, creative or repetitive. The adjustment comes naturally, is almost automatic. What works—works; what doesn't—doesn't! No moral authorities or spiritual instructions are needed to see the light!

All advanced players had to work through those personal or spiritual issues. They get no longer angry when they lose; they no longer worry over what the other guy may do or give in to unmitigated aggression in their attacks. They are rational and emotionally balanced people and they know themselves well.

The ability to feel deeply about life is directly proportional to the undoing of restrictive emotions like fear, aggression, impatience, arrogance or frustration! These emotions are not heart-based like feelings, but purely mental! They are a mental dysfunction that interferes with both reasoning and feeling. Chess clears these emotions and thus promotes emotional intelligence and the actual opening of the heart. It doesn't directly *do* it, but it makes ready for it.

Chess players are prepared to face their illusions, their prejudices and their life problems without being tempted to pull the avoidance trip. They practise this through every game. Illusion cannot persist against such regular acknowledgement.

Like the anonymous alcoholic, the player puts all his cards on the table and faces who he is. Or gives up chess...

I once asked the seventeen-year old star of our chess club, what goes through his head before winning all his championship games. "Do you so strongly want to win, or do you feel such complete confidence? What drives you, what makes you tick?" He answered without a pause: "I'm looking for the truth! The true next move, not tricks..."

I never forgot that and made it mine on the spot. After that, I took this pale, non-physical boy into high adventure to the Caribbean in exchange for daily games, where he ended up saving my life during a hurricane in Dominica, and eventually stayed hunting sharks for food...

"Manfix," as the Jamaicans called him, beat me in hundreds of games, with coal-black kids crawling all over us in bamboo jungle-huts, and girls rolling joints and their eyes at us—without ever giving me a single draw.

He later played chess for Germany for a bit, while studying philosophy, and basically kept travelling on shoestring all his life... But I made him my "guru" of the month then, for that statement about the true move. He was so right. It works...

It is valuable to understand what drives people like that...I saw Manfix go from boy to man in those four months; from a boy who couldn't gut a fish to a man surviving pirates and hurricanes and organising rescues in midst of six-thousand dead and many more damaged and injured people... He simply made the true moves all the time as he was used to do...

I'm still completely committed to the "true move," particularly as a parent! Tricks and traps may come up, but to seek them out loses more than it gains. There is no purpose or sense in creating illusion deliberately. Illusion is everywhere already... The best we can do is not to fall for it ourselves and to accept and speak nothing but what is true and real!

The difference between truth and illusion is easily seen by staring at a thing! Illusion disappears the more you stare at it. Truth however prevails and reveals ever new layers of deeper insight the longer you stare...

Observe that which *is* with courage and gratitude—that is the simple path to those deepest truths that cannot be directly taught.

And this is what we must, by example, cultivate in our children, if they are to reach their potential and build a better world.

Or maybe truth and honesty are among those things that our children are supposed to cultivate in us? So that we may finally grow up?

Chapter 3: Commitment and Observation

When beginners, and even quite advanced players play chess, they generally focus on trying to think and on formulating a plan. This is a fundamental mistake that also happens to parents that overthink and act upon a preconceived plan that keeps them from acute observation.

Thinking is such a vague word and we never ask ourselves what thinking and concentration actually entail and how to go about it.

When I started playing competitively, I used to sit there with my head held between my hands and trying to think as hard as I could. Of course, like anybody else, I thought through every move several times, forgetting what I had already resolved, struggling to make some clever plan, finding some trick and going through it all again, finally moving hastily when time demanded it. I worried about making mistakes that could impact on the chances of my team, and about my girlfriend who hated spending game nights alone.

At the end of a game, I used to have a head twice its former size and weight and I went to bed still full of unfound moves I should have made and didn't and my brain unable to stop thinking, even into my dreams. I often woke up having dreamed the elusive move and then played it out on the board before being able to sleep for real. I was a thinker.

My "commitment" consisted in winning for the club and in sitting there with my head swelling up. It was hard work, and I had a ceiling I could not break through.

I was a head-centred person. Then this all changed dramatically.

I travelled to Thailand with a friend, and we ended up in Koh Samui where one morning we had mushroom omelettes in "Munchies" restaurant before going to our favourite haunt. There was coffee and several chess boards, so we started playing while watching the droplets of crashing waves fill with stars and sunlight...

My friend reckoned there must have been a magic ingredient in our omelette, and I suspected the mushrooms. Unable to think in the usual linear way, I stared at the board as one would at a painting, purely observing what there was and gradually forgetting me, the observer. I did not "think" three moves ahead then, but rather watched the proceedings like a movie, where every move was a picture, a scene, all adding up to an unfolding future, a new landscape. It was utterly effortless to do so and the "film" easily went for seven or eight moves before getting fuzzy.

Other travellers sat down with us and I ended up playing on several boards simultaneously. It was still effortless to watch the "movies," so I ended up playing two players blind and simultaneous. I won every game. Suddenly the sun went down and the day was over! My head was clear, fresh and its normal size. We spent the night with some local girls and there was no chess flashback of any kind... Since that day I have always played chess like watching a movie. I never needed those mushrooms again to learn how to get into that same state of mind they seem to open up a gateway to. I don't "think" chess any more. I purely observe what goes and what does not.

Pure observation is something modern man has become near incapable of, since judgement is always jumped to prematurely, and we all see merely what we expect to see or are looking out for or are socially conditioned to see.

Pure observation is taking inventory only, seeing all that is actually there for what it really is. It is how children learn...

You look at a bishop in terms of its function, not just its shape—seeing all the open roads it can take, and those blocked by pawns. You feel the pressure it exerts down those roads and the threat to any other pieces in its way. There is no thinking to it.

You feel the pressure and the functions by simply looking at them with the commitment to finding truth.

A knight at the centre of the board, with six different fields to move to, feels strong and dangerous and puts pressure on all those fields, while a knight sitting on the side line feels weak, useless, inflexible and out of place. You see this by looking, not by thinking!

The act of pure observation is the same thing as meditation. It is an error to believe that meditation requires a lotus position or closed eyes or a quiet environment. To meditate is simply to commit to observing what is, and to be aware of IS-ness without sleeping or thinking it to pieces.

You can meditate during a boxing match or while playing volleyball or during your teenager's screaming session ...To purely observe, we just need to momentarily let go of expectation, prejudice, programming, and all other thought—like wanting to win or to outwit our opponent...

This is very difficult for modern man, although it is easier for children, when they are not yet hardened into their parents' prejudices.

Since my childhood, I had never really completely observed any more, and instead substituted it with "thinking," until Koh Samui.

Pure observation of the here and now is the only reliable guide we have into the future! The future can be predicted and chosen only by being utterly clear of the present.

Once you observe and feel the pressure on a pawn, you will want to alleviate that pressure in the future— what do you do?

Thinking hard of a way out will give you a headache, because trying to "think" five moves ahead creates time and obstacle and the resistance against it. The way to do it is to see the developing game as a film you merily watch, where every move creates a new picture and just as in animations—many pictures make a movie...

There is always a road for a misplaced knight to faint here and evade there, to manoeuvre into a good, strong position where it is most powerful. This visualization of possible roads is effortless like watching a film and carries us to new positions that we either like or not. Depending on how we feel about the relative end of our film, we then choose the movie we want to live!

If the knight gets lost along the way, we may not choose that film, but if the roads all open up for us and the dangers recede—we may like that film, that potential future, and we invite it to come to pass. This is playing!

The weighing up, judging, and analysing associated with thinking is replaced by feeling and observation throughout. Is it wiser to take this pawn, or to walk past it? Watch the two films and pick which end you like better! Logic is just a word we attach to accurate observation, which is seeing all the connections...

Of course, if the variant we consider leads to the capture of the opposing queen, logic will tell us to go for it, but we can see that before thinking it...

This becomes very clear in blitz-chess, where a player simply has no time to run through logical thinking processes and relies instead on visualization and feeling and even instinct! He moves much like a cat hunts, and a thick aura of awareness then often hangs over the players, keeping an entire crowd of spectators spellbound...

So, what does it take to reach this acute state of pure observation?

First, we need to take responsibility and find the courage to face the truth of what *is*! This will peel off most illusions. And then—we need commitment! And faith!

To meditate or observe, we need to commit to the here and now – or we will swerve away thinking of other things. What we call focus or concentration is nothing but commitment! A great musician does not "focus" or "concentrate" on remembering his lyrics and notes—he meditates his performance! That is why it all flows in total harmony!

A guitarist never thinks about his chords; he listens to the sound. He is committed to listening! Chess is just like that and parenting too. And it can be learned quite effortlessly!

Feeling utterly relaxed but responsible, you look at the functions of your bishops. You can imagine sitting in a boat floating and eventually speeding down those open channels the bishops have available to them to explore. ...You observe and take note of what is going on to your left and your right and ahead, as you would in any landscape. Some things, like pawns, waiting beside the stream, may feel dangerous and threatening, while other landmarks, like towers, may be a fine treasure, may be goals to pursue. You don't enter those channels with a looming presence waiting at the other end. Unless you do!

When you have thus explored all possible canals as far as the boat of visualization can carry you, it will be quite clear to you where you most like to travel! It feels like the boat knows where to go all by itself, just following the changes in its environment...

Observation does not fight imagined obstacles as thinking does, nor does it struggle against buts and ifs—so it does not cost energy and leaves the player fresh throughout and after the game! Most importantly, it is not trapped by duality, does not think in terms of black and white— but considers the entire function on the board as one!

Pure observation is observation where the observer himself has stopped to impose his dividing illusions on the observed object. He cannot maintain prejudices, like believing a rook to be always worth more than a knight. He cannot remain divided, considering his own moves more important than his opponent's, nor can he be attached to material possessions.

A player suffering say from self-pity, cannot easily recover from being "victimized" by a strong opposing move.... His observation of the position's truth unfolding here and now would thus be tainted, and so he needs to first face the personal truth of seeing himself as a victim.

Pure observation occurs only when the observer has let go of his looking devices, his particular ways of looking, his fixed view-points, his fears and his wishful thinking, his size, his speed, his imagined needs. It is what makes a good parent and it is what makes a great student!

Observation cannot be "done"—it occurs when the observer is ready to relax and let go of himself. Only then can he commit enough to be really with it, to flow with the functions, beyond just seeing his self-projected mirror images...

As in meditation, the "beholder" himself must be in the eye of the watcher before any beauty out *there* can be seen or identified from within.

When I teach people chess, I always stop them as soon as I see their heads growing heavy, lines creasing their foreheads and smoke coming out of...well, that's how it looks, when you can almost hear the ticking of their mental engines. "Stop thinking, mate!" I will say. "Just look at what there is and be with it!" They learn much faster that way.

Children should be shown chess-pieces and the ways they move very early, without further instructions or talk of winning and losing. A kid who learns to visualize early will be vastly more successful in all other areas of life! It is exactly as it is with mathematics—kids need playful, physical contact with geometry while they are very young, in order to get the abstractions of maths later. Oregami folding-techniques and platonic bodies, even a ball, will introduce them splendidly to maths, as they waken the senses that open to a commitment to observe. Chess is even more multi-dimensional, touchable and visual, and much more interactive.

I noticed many years ago, how kids from remote mountain villages in the Philippines, naturally endowed with a fresh jungle-intelligence, learn chess incredibly fast and to an astonishing level. They may not have higher IQs than western children in western tests, but their observation skills are vastly superior and so is their commitment to themselves and to family.

Pure observation is the most powerful tool on any worldly, scientific and spiritual path, and it needs to be taught as such to our young people! And to parents!

Is not observation the principal tool of the scientist as well? Does he not get his answers in terms of how acutely he looks at his experiment?

Does not quantum mechanics assert that the very act of observation actually changes the observed object? That all we see is determined by the way we look? Why aren't then scientists taught how to look and how to examine themselves, the observer...? Why aren't parents?

In my experience, chess makes observation, and specifically self-observation, more teachable than any other medium safely available in modern society, as it lends itself to self-reliant perception and to a commitment that is sorely lacking in other places.

And because all observations are so completely verifiable in chess, we can joyfully escape our democratic relativities and our uncommitted ambivalences here that keep truth well submerged in other fields.

Once you are committed to observation you will indeed know your child as she really is, not just what you would like her to be. And your children will learn through their own senses and experiments, rather than having to "believe" whatever they are told while becoming bored and uncommitted.

Chapter 4: Courage and caution

From the top branches of the mighty totara-tree comes the distant voice of my four-year old adventurer: "Da-ad, look how high!" I watch the skinny twigs bend, while she reaches higher still and my heart whimpers inside me, the protector. What should I do? Call her down, "right now!" to avoid a possible heart attack? Explain to her in a serious voice why this is too dangerous for a little girl...?

This is a sure way to instil fear, lack of self-esteem, lack of confidence and courage in both your kid and yourself!

Why not show them the difference between a dead branch that may break and the living one that will hold, by letting them try it out closer to the ground? That's what I did and then I let them live it up, up there with the unworried and melodious tui-birds, proud to have conquered a world all their own! This made me stronger and gave me trust and it helped my ability to let go of interfering. Not to mention what it did for my little monkeys...

One of the gravest errors in child-raising today is our reluctance to let kids take a risk and explore their boundaries! We overprotect them to death! We give them vaccinations against the flue, measles and rubella, which otherwise would serve to build a powerful immune system in children, and we give them antibiotics for ear infections that ribwort plantain would fix in a day, without side-effects. They must not touch fire, knives, dogs or anything with teeth, prickles or edges that might give them a life experience! We are raising fearful, incompetent children, and particularly our girls we protect from every challenge that nature has to offer and that might challenge their self-image of being a sweet, cute little princess enough to actually grow up.

I let my girls chop wood with an axe, never vaccinated them and never gave them any antibiotics or paracetamol, although doctors often called me a bad parent for it. We just laugh about people scared of the flue! Now they don't get the flue at all, having acquired massive immunity. They never fell out of a tree neither, nor did they chop their legs off...

Does this mean I'm a less cautious father than I should be? Quite the opposite! Caution is not the opposite of courage, but a necessary part of it! Caution is not in avoiding all dangerous situations but to avoid the dangers *in* these situations.

Not to use the axe is fear and self-doubt, not caution. Only by using it can they develop real caution! You just let them watch you do it and then take it careful step after careful step! This is only so hard to accept because parents are so very stuck in our own fears, never willing to confront them...We don't trust our kids any more than we trust ourselves, often even less!

Parents, who don't have the nerve to allow their children to swing the axe or take any dangerous risks, are well advised to introduce their little adventurers to chess!

It is interesting how a game of chess carves out the character of a person—some players may attack wildly with their queen, not caring if they end up losing her in the process, and others wall themselves into defensive positions without any cause, not daring to think offensively. As in life, so in chess, always!

Any strong player knows that courage without caution will lead to an "accident" just as surely as having caution without courage. The choice is between falling out of the tree and suffocation...

Apart from mirroring character and attitude, chess also forms character and adjusts attitude! It directly fosters cautious courage.

Being courageous requires a lot more caution than always to avoid danger, and that is why children allowed to take a risk are far more careful and cautious people throughout their far more courageous lives!

Once you have lost that queen enough times in wild attacks, you soon adjust to a more cautious approach in your attacks, which in time becomes a character adjustment towards reality and balance. Good chess players are neither too courageous nor too cautious.

When talking about courage we too often think of boys only, since girls' courage appears to be of a lesser importance. This is a huge mistake!

We are living in a time, where women are fast losing the courage and the ability to give unassisted natural births! Half of the new mothers now fear pain and natural processes to an extent that they have their babies cut out of them, just to avoid the natural experience! By far most of the rest prefer to dream away semi-conscious on epidurals, flooding their babies with toxic chemicals that cause a decline in immunity and in clarity of the senses. Most of us now enter this world in a hazy chemical fog, our kidneys burdened with the unexpected task of ridding us of toxins for months to come. The real horror here is not even the factual situation, but the vehement rejection western females feel towards even tolerating to hear any critique of that!

A male midwife in Australia has recently suggested just this and he was torn to shreds by every female with a mouth, including the NZ news speaker. "You just don't criticize the fairer sex" was the final, quite serious comment.

Since the first steps to finding courage are to take responsibility and to face truth, this should not surprise...

The answer here is not really to have a "natural birth" in the ocean, with dolphins for midwives. Better to book a hospital bed just in case, and then arrange for a doctor to wait outside your home with oxygen handy. This precaution taken, you have a homebirth in your own environment with a well-chosen midwife who might have skills in acupuncture, massage or hypnosis. The mother is in charge and has the actual experience. This is cautious courage.

Very few "mature" women today want to hear this though, as they haven't ever taken the humble first steps. They may not feel responsible or in their power enough to give unassisted birth but prefer instead to delegate the responsibility to doctors and hospitals. They don't face the truth as to the consequences and thus increasingly lack the courage women have had since the beginning of time—to be in charge of themselves! This loss of true woman-power far outweighs any political gains made by theso-called women's "liberation," and usually puts a male doctor in charge of what it is to become a mother.

In chess, there is no avoidance or delegation. There is true autonomy! We are responsible for all that happens, facing the hard truths of our own incompetence and opinionated prejudices, and we take charge of our destiny! In chess there is no sexism, no bullshit.

Chess fosters cautious courage to a point where girls will drop their princess status and challenge themselves to pull their own cart! Not many girls are able to learn this after the time they reach seven, after being pampered and protected into assimilating their parents' cute delusions. But a girl learning chess at age three does not easily go down that road and is just as competent later as any boy! It is not brain size which keeps girls out of chess clubs or from competing equally with male players. It is the way we raise them!

All the fashionable talk about "equality" is just talk, unless this is understood and until equality of responsibility, truthfulness and courage are part of the equation. Only then can what a woman observes on a chess board have "equal" accuracy and equally translate into daily life and into the courage of actually being a woman, instead of just a "lady."

To bring girls to the chess board can be tricky but is ultimately intensely rewarding. It is a great fathering tool and it keeps the wandering left brain better connected when oestrogen strikes...

On a spiritual level, courage is an indispensable quality, without which no progress can be made. To observe what we truly need to see is courage! To question our prejudices we need courage, and even to love we need a lot of courage. Nobody can learn to really love without courage. Those who think they "love too much," simply lack caution!

There can, of course, be no truth without courage, and no commitment to the chosen path.

Any gambit is an act of courage, where we rely more on our understanding than on material possessions. The King's Gambit is such an opening of courage and the mark of a courageous player. But what we need our guts for most is for letting go of "thinking" and to commit to seeing all there is to see without premature opinion or judgement.

As parents, this insight enables us to play successfully the gambit of letting our kids have their own experiences without constant interference, and to develop what our fearful hearts and our kids need most—trust!

Chapter 5: Having and losing

Another major factor to disrupt social and spiritual progress in the industrialized world is our predisposition for "having." We are consumers before we are anything else! Fears, unhappiness and boredom are dealt with by "shopping therapy;" our main drive has become greed, as Plato wisely predicted for all democracies, and who we are is most commonly reflected by the price and model of our car and other "status symbols" we acquired to make ourselves feel like "somebody." All areas of our lives are affected by this conditioning to *have* things rather than to *be* or to *give*. We *have* sex rather than *give* it, we *have* children and partners, we even *have* a toast instead of eating toast. It penetrates all of our thoughts, drives our careers and if we fail to subscribe to this strange philosophy, we become "losers..."

This "evolution" towards *homo consumeris* is what we call "progress," but progress towards what—remains the horrifying unasked question.

Does your child keep harassing you in shops with all the things she wants? Does she demand branded clothes, three-hundred-dollar shoes and the toys "everybody else" has? Are you falling for it? Are you raising a "have all you can" little monster?

What can the individual do who does not wish to join this race of rats and who might have as a goal in life to improve himself, rather than the material world our technology seeks to improve instead? – Live in a cave? Become a terrorist? A bum? A laissez-faire parent?

Is there any escape back towards sanity? What would convince us that "having" is not *it*?

It is quite possible to realize that having does not work for us. People like Bill Gates do realize that money cannot make happy or buy true joy. They tried it out. Most of us haven't, so we cling to the illusion that joy is just a lotto-win away.

The best way to realize that "having" is a very temporary thing of little substance is—losing!

Losing teaches the relativity of having, its temporary nature and its delusive quality! But losing hurts and we avoid it like a disease. Our children grow up either feeling like losers or in a race towards having what is not truly worth having.

Chess makes losing acceptable, bearable and valuable! But best of all, it teaches having and losing as a pair of connected principles that reveal superbly how it all works.

Having and *losing* seem to be opposites where the one implies and provokes the other. Without having, we can't lose, and the feeling of loss is always the other side of feeling we own something. Like our children, when they leave your home...It is not love, but the illusion of ownership that makes parents suffer and feel they are losing their kids, when they move on with their own lives or have their own minds.

The more we have, the more we can lose and the more we fear loss. The bigger problem however is our loss of direction in life from *having* and the blindness it causes towards all things that cannot be owned! Like children!

Having is the shortest path into deep illusion where impermanent things like cars have very high "value" while permanent things like our ability to love or to let go have very low value. It is not at all a matter of taste or opinion, what value a thing has, since true value is not determined by the "market forces" of supply and demand. The true value of any given thing is determined by its ability to help us on the path to realize who we are, where we are going and to what purpose. A car may advance us quickly to a different point in geography, but that point is usually no better at developing our humanity than the one we are presently at...

It is very different with a permanent thing like acceptance of *what is*. If you attain that, all your resistance and struggles against reality are over and your happiness improves vastly.

The values we attach to things have become grossly unreal and distorted because we have in fact lost our ability to value anything or to even understand value. We believe, according to supply and demand, that the more people seek a thing, the higher its value. In truth, it is the other way around: what most people seek are the trivial, temporary things that promise instant satisfaction. Those things with real value are sought, and even thought of, only by the few, never the many!

We have no sensible criteria as to what we should desire and instead let the advertising industry make those decisions for us, content to eat anything with a familiar plastic wrap. We have become pitifully poor people who not only don't have what they really need but have little clue that it may even exist.

And every time we buy much advertised things for our kids—we avoid giving them those things of real value that cannot be bought...

When people begin to play chess, they share all those same illusions and will apply them to their game. They don't understand the value of their pieces and believe that the outcome of the game depends on how many pieces they have lost or won.

Everybody raised in a consumer society initially shares those same illusions on the chess board! It is simple maths to them: a rook is worth five pawns. A bishop, or a knight, is worth 3.5 pawns. So, if the knight manages to go forward and fork the king and a rook, it will win a rook, while probably the knight won't survive. Five pawns worth of rook minus 3.5 pawns worth of knight—a net gain of 1.5 pawns, called a "quality." So, they go for it every time!

Now—what is the illusion in this? Well firstly, you cannot attach a fixed value to rooks or knights or anything. 5 and 3.5 are only statistical averages! The real value of a rook is determined from move to move, by the overall position! If all roads are nailed tight and the rook is immobile, its value may become less than one pawn. But if, in the end, all roads are open and the rook the only piece left, it will be sufficient to check-mate the king and win the game! Here its value is maximal. The rook can then do the same job as the queen and there is then no difference in value between rook and queen! The value here is—entirely relative to the goal, the check mate.

Sometimes, a knight can check- mate, where the queen can't. Is the queen then still worth more? Certainly not! The knight is then infinitely more valuable than the queen!

Pawns can also increase in value by becoming "free" pawns or by getting ready to convert. Their value is never fixed, but always given by the potential function towards a goal.

Secondly, value is determined by kinetic energy. If a knight has already taken three moves to stalk into a prominent forward position, it is worth more than an undeveloped knight, simply because we have invested three moves (tempi) in it already. A knight so advanced is often worth more than the locked-in rook in its corner, that it plans to swap for after the fork.

What we find out, bit by bit, is that *having* in chess (and life) isn't what it is cracked up to be! We're chasing after an idea to win a pawn or bishop and succeed, but suddenly we have arranged all our material on that side of the board, far too occupied with gleeful feeding, while on the other side, the opposing forces go about the business of mating our king...

Even if we manage to "win" a rook, this does not mean at all that our chances of winning the game have improved. Often, we lose much tempo or connectedness over our material gain, which can outweigh the material possessions completely.

Therefore, employing this in reverse, we may sometimes ignore an attack on our pieces, even sacrificing the queen in order to gain time to go about a check mate without the queen! A sacrifice is a letting go of material possessions for the sake of pure idea or the freedom to move unhindered. To detach oneself from one's lovely queen and other treasured possessions so as to be exactly where one needs to be, is a spiritual ability never cultivated in a consumer-society and therefore only very advanced players will be able to see such choices.

To become a good chess player, it is necessary to detach from materialism to the point where giving up the queen is always an option, and where an attack does not necessarily require a defence. As long as we seek to chase and eat pieces for their substance, we are chasing illusions. It simply isn't about eating more pieces than the other feller...

A great beauty about chess is that it is a powerful statement against the philosophy of materialism, which is now the new world religion. We can figure out quite easily that a materialistic approach does not work. A good player can always prove to a beginner, that he can give two rooks and a bishop handicap and still win, because he achieves more function with a knight than the beginner with his queen...Children quite quickly pick this up and learn the relativity of *having* and the dangers of consumerism.

Idea replaces material. I played a game once, where I had sacrificed all my pieces to suffocate the opposing king at the centre of the board and check-mated him there with a lonely pawn...I was flooded with serotonin and dopamine and unadulterated joy from this delightful mate...

What great beauty lies in giving up everything and to win by the sheer virtue of keeping only what is necessary, while the opponent breaks down under the weight of having too much and no freedom to enjoy it in!

All chess players love a good sacrifice, especially where they can see what they will later get for it in return...But there are so-called "genuine sacrifices," where you can't see the reward, but trust some gut-feeling or instinct, or sense of time, to get your reward eventually. Here your trust is quite general, that time and idea will out-trump material—a most spiritual attitude.

In openings, this giving up of possessions for quality of movement is quite institutionalized and we call this a "gambit." We say—here is this pawn—undefended and generously offered—take it! Eat it! We don't care! It was only in our way! Eat!

Apart from it being good psychology, this is a truly empowering attitude to take! It is the antithesis to our collectively shared conditioning to be consumers and materialists!

I love gambits, especially the king's gambit, dangerous though it may seem. It gets people going! Greedily they come swinging and pillaging. After all, they're already ahead by a pawn...

You let them lunge forward, swivel a bit, like a tai chi master, letting them continue with their own momentum of feeding frenzy, until they overextend themselves and—disintegrate. They die from greed, from consuming too much, from carrying too much weight...

A genuine sacrifice is like a fast that leaves you mean and lean, or like a business slimming down in order to become more efficient in its operations. Playing a gambit is inviting a player to be a materialist and then proving him wrong...

This is exactly what little kids need to learn before they become a nuisance in shops! You could show them how you can get a dog to drop the big bone it carries by offering him a smaller one, and how to buy brand clothes for two dollars at a garage-sale! If they want expensive blueberries, give them a couple of plants to grow them!

In chess, when a piece is dangled in front of our greedy little mouths, or a queen is asking to be ravished, we are well advised to first inspect ourselves, our hunger to succeed, our illusions of "having" —before we start snapping up our pound of flesh! We need to keep in mind the higher purpose of the game, instead of wolfing down everything coming our way, looking pretty...

Good examples are the Middle Gambit, where you need to stop eating pawns lest the foray leads you into the desert; or the variant in

Bird's opening – f4-e5, fxe-d6, where continuing to feed gets you under an early and dangerous attack.

Don't eat just because it's there! You might get overweight!

Eat only, where eating strengthens your purpose!

On the other hand, don't wait for the wolf to come on you unawares. Feed it! Bait the wolf to come exactly where and when you expect it to come. By feeding the wolf you know where he is, where he will be and you know his plan! It is much wiser to feed the wolf a poisoned chunk of bishop than hiding behind a wall where you can't see the prowling wolf.

"Having" comes to a bitter end very easily, often just because of a loss in flexibility, but usually because we attach to much value on possessions, which blinds us to function.

All having brings with it losses. While you are having a meal, or look proudly at your new car, time goes by while you become stationary and predictable and a target for the flies and the thieves, the hungry and the poor and the jealous.

Everything you have cost you a price and keeps on costing it, unless you focus on function!

Having is also often unnecessary. Why bother to take a rook which is completely blocked in, unable to move any time soon? It has no function, no value, so why bother "having" it?

It can be a great advantage if the opponent has some material left, as it can prevent a stale-mate and even help you when check-mating him. You cannot check-mate a naked king with only two horses, but you can do it sometimes with only one horse, so long as the opponent still has a side-pawn. The true value of things is only in their function, not their structure or in their cost.

Losing is the nature-given therapy for having! Players, who like to "have" a lot—will naturally lose a lot.

A society oriented around "having" creates many losers, and so do games of chess, only here the cause-effect relationship is far more visible and quite reversible.

In a real sense, chess has no losers at all. That is if we gain a precious learning experience from every game, no matter the outcome! How can the outcome of a game influence how much we gain and learn, or how much beauty we experience? It doesn't.

Chess is entirely about the path, even if it has a goal, and every game, like a new incarnation of our deepest beliefs, confronts us with our inner selves and our illusions. This brings us new insights and new losses.

The experience of losing is of course the antidote to our attachment to having and spiritually; to lose is actually more profitable than to win for most people, most of the time.

Particularly parents have a lot to lose, like their fears and prejudices and eventually—if they hold on to them too much—their children.

Taoist thought sees advancement not in gaining new knowledge, but in emptying oneself of the false and the unnecessary. Losing is like emptying the ego, like stripping away pretence, arrogance and poor judgement, attachments and false beliefs, until we can see clearly what truly *is*. Losing well can be an art and a very profitable business to the parent seeking to distil essence.

Hence, the Tao-Te Ching tells us in chapter 42:

.....for one gains by losing

and loses by gaining...

What the Hindu calls "maya" and the Mexican Indian "tonal," which is the world of illusion—must be shed in order to know the truth! Chess is much like that and so is parenting!

By far the most engrained of our illusions, "having" has confused us individually and collectively to the point of severe addiction. It has led science to see mind as having evolved from matter and physical symptoms as being quite unrelated to emotions and thought...It distorts and sabotages medicine, physics, economics and of course our ability to live in peace. And "having" is the primary example we daily set to our kids, who can soon not stop thinking of what to want next...

Is there a way out?

Naturally, you can give all your money away and join some "religious" group. Or go cave-hunting. Or get sick enough. Or you could give your kids all the toys and brand-clothes you can afford and see what you find out, when your child becomes your mirror...

However, if you buy your family's clothes at garage-sales, you hone your kid's observation- and evaluation- and negotiation-skills on this discovery-trip, and you also save so much money, you need to work less and have more time with your kids! If you select quality clothes, wash, sun-dry and then adjust to purpose, your kids will wear only the best. After buying brand dresses from other kids who had grown out of them, for fifty cents, they develop a good sense for money and soon feel "sorry" for those who buy them for three hundred dollars in fancy shops. Eventually they'll clean out all their old treasures in a garage-sale of their own and make a profit getting rid of what they no longer need...

Or they can play chess, where "having" will regularly reveal itself as illusion, where losing becomes a pain-free practise and where all you "have" after a game, all that truth and beauty you walk away with—can never be lost.

Chapter 6: Doing and Being

When my girls went to karate tournaments, I used to tell them what to look out for and what to do against specific opponents. "Watch out for those high kicks to the right side of your head!" "Keep your fists higher and watch your footwork!" And worst of all: "watch what you are doing!" This never worked... Bang! Here comes the kick to the left side of her head...

Also, when playing chess, to warn them not to lose their queen would achieve just that.

When I had finally observed the mechanics of this, I gave up telling them what to do and not to do. "Just be yourself! Self-responsible as the beast in the jungle!" worked a lot better and saying nothing worked best.

I then noticed, that they quite generally didn't want to be told what to do, not because of any rejection of authority, but because it didn't work for them to think about the doing of it.

We may have "done" a fair bit of travelling together, to remote and wonderful places, but we never had a real plan for what we would do when spending four months on a jungle island. We never pre-booked a room or planned our daily activities. We were just there, in some village, in paradise, and that was enough. When there were kayaks, we would try them out and when we felt like island-hopping, we jumped a boat leaving at that time. Our days were always unplanned and we just lived there, happily being alive.

Unfortunately, pure being outside a simple native society has become a thing of the remote past and is lost to memory. We are what we "do." We are a baker, a builder or a teacher and ask each other—how do you *do*?

And when we travel, everything is pre-planned, all rooms booked in advance, every day's activities worked out weeks earlier and everything well insured...

This is how we lose our ability to simply *be*.

Even when ill, we take some "paracetomol" or migraine tablets and keep on doing, instead of accepting nature's suggestion and just *be* sick for a couple of days, doing nothing.

Like first-child parents, people starting to play chess will of course follow their entrenched habits and apply all their obsessive "doing" to the chess game. They will make plans for how to "win" and wonder what their opponent might have "planned." They try to set traps and invent tricks and are determined to overwhelm their partner with the clever things they do.

When I asked Manfix about this, he but smiled manfixishly and asked back "Why would you want to trick anybody or try attacking him for no reason? Let the other guy do all that and then allow the truth to prove him wrong!"

I found his way of looking at chess extremely enlightening and applied his mango-induced statements successfully in this and other areas of life.

While a game is still in balance, there is nothing to do but observing what is and to go with it, avoiding over-sights. To try and trick the opponent will always give you a weakness, unless the "trick" is not intended and just comes up with observation. When you try a "trick," you are hoping your opponent falls for the trap instead of seeing the truth of it. Your "doing" is then nothing but wishful thinking, much like lottery. It makes you a poor parent and a poor player at any game.

A trick or trap you intend, will usually backfire and reveal the lack of complete observation. Tricks are a product of desire, of wanting to win and score and thus have limited focus. We try to force the issue of winning. But it is quite silly to impose one's will, hope or desire on a well-balanced position! Attacking, when there is no weakness and no ground, cannot work.

It is much like ten soldiers trying to take a solid position by storm that is well defended by also ten soldiers. A bad plan! It is better to wait for the right opportunity. Better, to hold the peace until a wall crumbles or half the defenders are out of ammo. To attack without call is a mistake that has lost many a game…

We cannot *do* anything against a solid defence. We need to manoeuvre in our own space, just being present, flexible, efficient, patient and happy, until things change. Only when the opponent loses patience and overextends himself, will there be a weakness inviting an advance. But then we don't have to do it so much as to simply reflect this weakness in an increasing strength of our own, and like water we can then flow into the opening vacuum.

Imagine a tai chi master. Would he run at a person and start swinging? Never! He stands there, at peace, no intent, no thought of a fight. When he is attacked, he may not even oppose that force, but let it harmlessly flow past him. Only when the attacker over-extends and struggles for balance, the master will gently guide him even more out of balance and then allow his own motion to take the attacker down.

This is exactly how to play chess, or for that matter—how to conduct a hard business negotiation and how to "deal with" difficult children…The more we *do*, the more we will struggle!

The tai chi master never struggles, never tries (God does not particularly love a tryer!), he never imposes, never "does." He simply *is*. Like water! Just like the effective parent!

Is your kid "hyperactive" and has short attention spans? He may have already learned your and your culture's obsession with doing, or his own action is restricted to mental doing, while natural physical activity is suppressed. Activity and even work do not have to be a "doing" in this sense of mental, fidgety unease. Work is the result of your interaction with the world, but "doing it" is resisting the pleasure and the ease of it! "Hard work" is struggling and resisting! Work becomes very easy when it is lived instead of done. Enjoyed instead of suffered!

Just watch young kids playing before and after they get seriously told what to do, to see this!

The performance of a rock star is not a doing and neither is the best work of a counsellor, a teacher or a sex-worker. Even a builder knows how effortless building his own home is compared to building somebody else's, according to their plans and instructions. He also knows how the hand can, without any "thinking," nail up a wall in no time and how days can fly with good work mates for company...

You've certainly tried out "doing" as a parent! Made a plan, set standards, visualized your kid's future, including their likely career, and then went about implementing it? Used psychology! Science! Praise and punishment! Told them where to go and what to do...

One should think that such experiments prove futile so quickly, that no parent would do it a second time, but this is strangely not so! We rather insist on what we are trying to "do," justifying it and we ask each other—what more can I "do?"

We rarely learn from our experiences with children, since we have decided that it is only them who need to learn from us, and that we are always right as parents. In chess, these escapes do not work!

Doing does not work with children or for the fighter, the singer or the chess player.

Why not just *be* with our children more, letting go of the inner race, sing more in the shower—and remember how to play...?

And when playing chess, we need to let go of the winning/losing trip and the constant need to "do" something about it! We need to relax and enjoy what we see...we need this ability when our kid plays risky games and shows us like a mirror that we can do nothing at all! That we are now helplessly facing what our kid does...

At chess, "doing" is just as deadly. A game never follows any one player's plan anyway since we can't predict our partner's next move. It gradually takes on shape, growing from indistinct potentials in the opening to take on definite structure in the middle game. We may try to steer clear of the rocks, but the game's dynamics pull us along like a river, opening up new vistas, dangers and opportunities, that we can either see—or not.

A good wood-carver does it the same way when he looks at a piece of gnarly peach—he does not impose his ideas but looks for what shape might be hiding in his chunk of wood. He chisels away the soft and rotten parts, going with the grain, chips away the unnecessary and comes to discover eventually the shape inherent in the wood. What his hand does simply follows his inner eye and the grain obediently and without additional "doing".

This is what Lao-Tzu means when he declares in Tao-Te-Ching, chapter 48:

"In the pursuit of learning, every day something is acquired.

In the pursuit of Tao, every day something is dropped.

Less and less is done until non-action is achieved.

When nothing is done, nothing is left undone."

In chapter 69 he almost seems to be talking about chess:

"There is a saying among soldiers.

I dare not make the first move but would rather play the guest.

I dare not advance an inch but would rather withdraw a foot.

This is called marching without appearing to move,

Rolling up your sleeves without showing your arm,

Capturing the enemy without attacking,

Being armed without weapons..."

This Taoist wisdom incidentally also describes the perfect attitude parents should cultivate if they wish to fully enjoy the fruits of parenthood! "Doing" loses as many chess-games as it loses opportunities to simply be with your kid without a mental agenda.

Openings like "French," "Pirc," and "Caro Kann" apply the principle of not making the first move towards an attack. Here the player plays the guest, who will not advance or show his arm. He holds back all doing, observes and waits for the right time.

Even when the time comes to embark on a wonderful combination, or when a "plan" unfolds, he will not do more than observe, be aware, without adding to what he sees.

In the endgame, there is even less sense in any "doing." It is all about seeing. When there is a five-move forced mate on the board, what is there to do? It is just a matter of seeing it! The hand is ruled by the eye. No decisions or plans are to be made, no actions thought of.

We simply see the truth of it—and nothing is left undone.

Children know all that and express it when playing—before we consistently query them on what they would "like to do" and judge what they have done.

Doing is related to thinking in that it isn't happy with what is but needs to get somewhere else constantly. It is doing what separates us from living the moment here now, from understanding children and from divine happiness! Doing keeps us from realising who we really are and accepting it. It keeps us from finding God. From knowing our children! From seeing what's on the board...

Doing is why seekers don't find God! We suppose God to be somewhere else, above the clouds or beyond this world or after death but above all—hiding! So, we do all these things, like looking in books for "him," confessing our "sins," feeling guilty, or praying for salvation or saying mantras.

But the truth is that God does not hide! She is here, now, accessible, obvious and manifest in this world. She is in Nature and in our inner natures. She is life and breath and she is who gave us our children, not Mendel.

To experience God, we need not do anything but accept being and to see clearly what there is to see. There is no merit in chasing the idea of a hidden God!

Imagine all religious fundamentalists, Christian, Muslim and Jew, dropping all they are doing now, all their useless rituals, their violent "doings," their exclusive assertions, their disrespectful missionaries. Would that not clear their eyes for being more human and more real? Would that alone not help them to find the very thing all their doings have blinded them for?

The philosophy of non-doing is very difficult to adopt in our frenzied environment unless it is actually tried out. Only some artists and musicians and of course tight-rope walkers seem to discover it and are promptly considered "superstars" by an astonished public.

Love-making would also greatly benefit from an approach of being, rather than doing, as any woman will confirm with that long-held sigh...

Doing is what destroys sex, parenting, wood-carving and spiritual quests in our time. It produces an aimless technology and harms our chances to reach our human potential.

Chess is in itself not necessarily conducive to non-doing. But it is the perfect instrument for observing how setting a trap leads us into the trap ourselves, and how doing and trying always throw us off balance. It teaches us that doing keeps us from seeing with clarity what already is, and that it simply does not work well with children.

In order to get good at chess and parenting, we have no choice but to let go of our fidgety selves, to forget our plans and concepts and to see what is right there in front of our eyes.

We then stop trying to "do" things that are not in the cards.

We will not move an inch forward unless a stumbling opponent offers us his space.

We do not show our arm. We practise non-action when our kids act out or over-react.

That is how we get the real work done.

That is the way to become a competent parent and to raise self-responsible and self-accepting children.

Chapter 7: Beginnings and endings

The saying—did you get up with the left foot? —implies that a day is usually only as good as we started it. This seems true for the night as well since—we "sleep in our bed as we made it."

Beginnings and endings define all things. Life is essentially defined by a person's birth and her death. It can therefore be best understood from the experience of birth and death.

That is why the neo-Reichian technique of rebirthing and a contemplation of death can bring such powerful benefits to the person on the path to cultivate undivided awareness.

However, as a culture we abhor both birth and death and refuse experiencing either. Mothers give birth in an epidural haze shared by their babies, neither living the experience, and death is similarly conducted with chemicals, so that we may fall asleep unwittingly rather than to let go consciously in the face of death.

And, of course, birth and death happen in institutionalized isolation, preventing most people from having seen a single birth or a death by the time they reach adulthood!

This has far-reaching and fundamental consequences to our sense of reality generally and to any evolution of consciousness in particular.

For our children, who are artificially kept away from experiencing birth or death, the psychological shortfall is disastrous! It is quite impossible to be prepared for life, or to have much sense for life, if you have never seen a woman giving birth and a person die...

Carlos Castaneda rightly calls death the "best adviser," because it is the judge over which things are permanent and which are not, which goals to aspire to and which not.

We can indeed understand life a lot better, when we have learned about birth and death as one, recalled our childhood and mastered the art of letting go.

For children a well-lived morning gives the pattern for the whole day and they won't need reminding to do things well or to wake up to reality. Equally, when you engage them in learning or work, ensure that they have a happy start based on choice and fun! You can then walk away and leave them to it! It is easier to be self-responsible while continuing to have fun after an exceptional beginning.

People, who understand a bit about life, start their mornings with an awareness of what matters in their day, which can become an effective and fruitful ritual to them. They may stretch, then get up, rub their eyes, drink a glass of water, do their morning gymnastics, have a shower, brush their teeth, have a shit and breakfast, and leave home when good and ready, and nothing missed or forgotten.

This is a much better opening to the day than scrambling for time, chasing the kids from the bathroom, instructing the wife to move faster and running to the car, pulling up the pants between gears...

As we try to have a good morning and to give our offspring a good start in life, so we also need a good opening for our game of chess. An opening like the release of an arrow...

What then is a "good" opening? A good opening is one that has always the end in mind—the check mate! Like the hunter, before he strikes out, will oil his gun, wax his boots, feed the dog and pack his provisions with the stag in mind, so the chess player too will "oil" his bishops by placing them on fast open roads, "wax" his king into a safe place, feed out some bait and pack his rooks into a neat stack, while dreaming of a good check-mate.

We then visualize and chase the game without stumbling into it, all the while using all of our skill, all our senses, all our provisions and tools. Our senses are wide open, while every part of us moves to its proper position, getting ready for whatever may happen.

Openings are not very tactical, not like the end game, where pure mathematical truth awaits discovery, leaving us no choice to create or be arbitrary.

Any pawn or knight can start the game; there is no "best" first move. No "best" opening. All the cat does is stretch itself...

There is a wide choice in taste or style as to how to open. What matters is not what opening we play, but how consistent our moves are, how connected with each other.

Like a youth or a baby, the opening looks with wide innocent eyes at the main game, expressing the nature of the player on his way to experience life. It can come to symbolize the character of a player and even become a personal pet like say a car.

The way people begin something can tell a lot about who they are. Accountants may be likely to favour the careful "French" opening or the "King's Indian," while adventurers might like the "King's Gambit," but it is more the particular and personal way a person plays and gets himself ready, that tells us the most about who he is.

To some people "getting ready" means an entirely different thing from what it means to others. Some want to first see their king safely tucked away, protected by sturdy formations of pawns, before they think of any foray, while others are quite ready to jump to the hunt, when they come across a stray horse close to their territory. Some only get one side of the board ready, others only two or three pieces.

There are two basic ways to play an opening: One way is to play for impetus and momentum, by gaining tempo during development, which is done by deploying all pieces economically and getting them into their optimum positions faster than the opponent. This means we don't move our pieces twice if it can be helped, we don't step into the path of our developing pieces and we don't allow them to be chased by a developing opposing force.

The other way is to let the opponent march forward while we wait in a defensive posture for him to attack too quickly or deploy his pawns in frontier country we control and where he can't defend them—as in "King's Indian" or "Pirc."

The principles of flexibility, connectedness and efficiency always apply, whatever we play, and grow into qualities of character in the young player.

And the reverse: It is likely that a "morning person" will play a better opening than a night-owl—and people who use rituals in preparation also do better at openings.

Kids who easily find good beginnings in chess, will start all else with the same confidence.

And then there is death. In endgames, we will only succeed if we like to bring a job to a good result, if we like a happy ending.

Endgames are the death and glory of a game, the physical death of each incarnation of the game and as such they are also the time of facing ultimate truth. What we have done throughout the game's life, all the mistakes we made, comes to haunt us now, forcing us to see the karmic fall-out. Or we have won a few skirmishes and a few pawns and now we have to show that this was enough to win the battle of yin and yang, wrapping it all up in the final conclusion. Knowing how to finish things is to know how to grow up...

There is little space for creation, choice or style in the end-game; it is all about seeing the truth and living by it. Flexibility and time are of relatively little importance at the end of game or life. It's about getting things done. Completed.

Can we end the battle? Everything takes its final shape, like the lines and wrinkles of an old man, his final posture, his last word. The count of the Fallen.

Old players are better at endgames than at openings, because they can better relate to the psychology of coming to the final conclusion and facing the final bill.

Players, who avoid the thought of death entirely, will struggle at endgames, at final outcomes and at objective reality.

In order to get good at this, we need to *like* endings, knowing there is never an absolute end to anything. Life has no real beginning and no real end. Neither has the universe.

There are only relative beginnings and endings, births, big bangs, decays and collapses.

The insights after a defeat become the beginning of a new game. Death is not permanent, which is why it makes sense to learn from it every time it happens. This is critically important for children to comprehend, as it prevents most fear of death and of life!

We begin a new game, conscious of how we lost the last one, and our new openings arise from the experience of previous death, just as our deaths are made and forecast by our openings.

An endgame is very much like dying. First, we lose flexibility and our movements slow down. We see less and less choices and no escape, no future. We shrink into a corner, our power shrivelling up with every move. Finally, we can't breathe, can't move and we can see it coming...this is how we die on the chess-board.

Chess can actually help a lot with dying, teaching us to accept death in our progression through all our losses on the board. And in reverse, those who have faced death of the physical body will have no pain when losing a game of chess, nor fear it.

All things are connected like this, even in reverse, and can be employed to shape our manifestations of change.

The "outcome" of a game is of course not just the check-mate. It is in all we learn and in the beauty of tactical combinations, the joy of seeking truth! The check-mate may not even be the ultimate goal for the self-developing player. But the check-mate gives us orientation, direction and makes it a game and a discipline.

Death is not our goal in life either. It just gives us orientation! It makes the game! Without death, life could not exist any more than left can without right.

Death defines the meaning of all the moves we make in life; it sets all the rules and the horizon for our worldly ambitions.

As much as a life is determined by the circumstances of birth and by the manner in which we face our death, so is a chess game defined by the opening and the resulting endgame.

To play a gambit in the opening is carrying our awareness of death from the beginning and to practise dying from the second pawn onward, in order to fuel life.

A player in fear of death would be uncomfortable losing a pawn straight away. He will protect all his precious pawns and possibly not even take what he is being freely given, for fear it may be poisoned...

Did you think you can successfully "raise" your child without easy and fearless lessons about death? Do you keep your child away from dying people, from "morbid talk," dead animals, and "protected" from your own fear of death? Know that a child cannot learn about life without facing death! Of course, it is not taught at schools how to face and understand death. None of the important things, like death, sex, spirit, initiations and all else that makes people break out in pimples, is a subject at school, and where else is a city-kid supposed to learn those fundamental things?

There is another, even less agreeable aspect to endings, the "doing" of death, which is—killing! In an endgame, the dominant player does not offer a draw. He goes for check-mate and for that he needs what we might call a killer-instinct. How does that sound in a peaceful Taoist context? Well, it sounds like real life...

Leave the glass houses of civilization and you can get killed in the jungle! If you don't kill first! That is reality. And you need to kill every time you want something decent to eat or set foot on the forest floor...

There is no butcher to do it for us. In nature, we take responsibility for ourselves and accept that killing simply *is*.

You can shoot a deer, cut its throat, drink its blood, be grateful to the deer—and yet be a highly evolved person! Just as the Native American tribes...

We all kill. We eat meat. We swat flies, we step on cockroaches, we throw atomic bombs and feel justified to do all that. What we haven't learned or long forgotten is to kill well, honestly and with respect! To self-responsibly kill a pig after a life-time of buying pork and bacon is neither "cruel" nor "violent," but necessary to a sane and honest character free of double-standards!

If you really want to allow your child to develop naturally, don't pretend that all killing is bad. Let your kid catch a fish, kill it, gut it and cook it, then eat it!

So, don't fret when you're only moves away from check-mating your partner and give him the quickest, cleanest death! This will honour your opponent.

Don't let him escape over and over, as the cat does to the mouse, or chase him across the board for extended humiliation. Give him a death that crowns his life and his game.

Make a good kill. Express your respect! Give him your beauty!

Find a good death!

Chapter 8: Strategic Parenting

Have you ever noticed how your sprat doesn't like to be told what to do or what to think? If yes, you have an intelligent child, congratulations! And you yourself are not stupid either, for observing this!

There are two basic ways a child will react to goals and imperatives his parents pursue in raising him to be a "good" person. Either he will be obedient and copy the parent well beyond his seventh year, thus becoming the "model son." Or he will refuse to walk his parents' trodden path and do exactly the opposite.

Kids, who think for themselves, and all the smarter ones, will tend to become the opposite of the parent whenever parenting imposes views that cannot be explored or challenged.

The more a parent pushes his views, the more opposition he will create. A boy, forced to go to church in suit and tie, by a Catholic father who tells him the stories about the virgin Mary and the infallible pope, will either never question things in his life, or awaken to the fact that his old man is an ignorant agent for the interests of the Catholic church, at the expense of honesty, truth and loyalty to his son! The resulting family conflicts are inevitable, because this father/son relationship is at an end! Trust gone. Check-mate!

Most parents' experiences with "unruly" children are created this way by the parent trying to rule them.

Parents most often don't encourage their kids to develop their own world view and instead program them to their own limited perceptions and cultural beliefs. This is why in NZ nearly all boys play rugby, trying to please their fathers' best hopes, and this is why boys in the US "like" baseball.

A Catholic is a Catholic because he is born and raised that way. There is no merit in that, surely. If you are born in Iraq, you will be raised a Muslim, and if you happen to be born in Israel, that'll make you a Jew. None of these so-called "faiths" are chosen by a free mind, nor are they the result of truth-seeking or of a developing intelligence.

A child born in the US will be raised to consumerism, to unrestrained growth (obesity) and to striving for financial success. This is not parenting, but blind and automated programming of children as we ourselves have been programmed! There is no responsibility in that and no respect!

Real parenting would encourage a child to question all those things like consumerism and what we call religion to a point where she is no longer manipulated by it! How else would intelligence develop? The cardinal strategic misadventure of parents has always been this enormous disrespect for the freedom and the uniqueness of the spirit they call "their" child! It simply does not work with bright kids to manipulate them, and hence the battle of the generations...

Oh, it works as far as we are concerned, if our own sheep-like child turns mini-me, but it does not work if you wish your child to develop her own intellectual and spiritual potential. And either way—it sure turns the parent into the enemy!

Every teenager smart enough to doubt and question will see through the agenda of the preaching parent eventually, and then fight him as the nemesis of his freedom and of self.

If authority does not come completely natural and does not arise as respect in the child as the giver of that authority—the parent becomes the opponent and the child no longer listens to a thing.

The strategic move for the enlightened parent is to show proper respect, to try and get over her own inner divisions and implanted beliefs—and to stop preaching! To stop feeding answers and instead keeping the questions alive! To show some humility and to admit to fallibility...

If you but show your child how you can drop your own arrogance and certainty—you begin to live the example for what human and spiritual path is all about and of what you wish your teenager to become capable of. If you but show true respect, your child will learn self-respect and respect of others, which is the backbone of all other virtues you can possibly strive to cultivate...

But if you demand to be respected more than you yourself respect your child—the moves to check-mate are countable...

It is sometimes said that children need not a friend, but a parent. I will agree that kids need much more guidance by example than they get today from a very few competent adults, and I strongly advocate more happy work, challenges, hardships, fasts, tasks.

But all this "guidance" needs to be by example, not words! The trouble with most parents is that they expect kids to do as they *say*—while kids ignore that and do what the parents *do*, which upsets the parents enough to blame the kids for doing what they themselves can't admit to doing and instead teach not to do.

Kids learn from what we do. Live with it!

The acute observer will realize that kids learn very much faster from other kids than from adults. Those other kids are their friends!

Other kids don't intentionally teach them, they simply are older and younger, stronger and weaker, nicer and meaner. This teaches a kid to look up in imitation, down in protectiveness, and all around in orientation. Playfully! This is how they learn best!

Those other kids are their friends! They are from the same planet!

They don't teach them, they can simply do, better or worse, developing the student- and the teacher-side of any kid without getting all mental over it as adults do.

It costs a lot of self-important pride for parents to accept such a humiliating fact and that is why they cannot see it, no matter how obvious.

There is nothing wrong with being your child's friend! Respect makes you a friend.

And how can you, without all that surrendered "authority" still give firm and strong guidance?

Authority is needed only where words replace example. Based on denial, it lives of being forceful, controlling and violent. Untrusting!

But if you teach by example, living a strong, virtuous, creative, happy and loving life under the eyes of your child, you will succeed as a parent—quite without any self-proclaimed parental authority or many wise words!

Is it not enough influence on your little girl to sometimes find you in serene meditation, in prayer, in contemplation of beautiful, small, and even invisible things?

Why does she need to be taught to kneel to an altar or veil herself or speak our words when listening to *her* Gods??

My primary advice to the emotionally challenged parent is this:

Don't become your child's opponent! If you already are, then get off your authority and control issues and restore mutual respect! How can you do that? You could row a boat with your son, for a week, in dangerous waters—that could do it.

You won't argue for very long, but you may drown before you respect each other...

If you hate drowning or getting wet, chess offers a wonderful path where you start in complete opposition and end up honest partners, capable of rowing a boat together and of understanding each other and your place in the family!

Try this one:

Sitting across a square table, you face your most merciless opponent—your son— over a chess-board. There is you and him, yin and yang, opposing world views and hostile generations, facing up to their irreconcilable differences in the perception of reality. It starts like a competition, where every move is a statement on what you and him each think is true and real.

But here now comes the strategic point—you speak aloud why you make your move, what your perception is and your very plan! Give away all your secrets, holding nothing back! "I'll try for your rook by marching this and that pawn, until your rook becomes fork-able..."

Then you encourage your son to also think aloud! To criticize your own thoughts and to propose better ones and a better plan! "I might let you go fork my rook, while I capture your queen," he might respond.

You very quickly learn to respect each other's truth this way and then you can watch those two truths converge towards objectivity...

Now, the arbiter over who is righter is no longer age, experience or authority, but instead clarity, reason and insight! Can you live with that? Your son most likely can.

If you want to see eye to eye with him again, here is your best chance.

Don't forget a "thank you for the game, mate" after you lost. Mean it!

What other strategies do you really need unless you just want to manipulate and program a child?

A girl who loves playing chess does not need further encouragement with math, science and self-motivated learning. She will love a challenge and enjoys getting better. She respects her chess-parent and is used to speaking her mind. She is confident and she has a tool for life to develop her character with, even when school lets her down.

The chess-parent remains part of her life and his advice is received happily.

He is not the opponent, the alien from another star-system, when she turns fifteen!

The cultivation of mutual respect is likely the best strategic move you will ever make and there is indeed no need for further strategic considerations.

All you really have to give as a parent is who you are, what you can express, how you honestly feel and think. And this conveys itself naturally to your child, without force or authority or doing, if it is at all worth having.

Children are not stupid, as some of us tend to believe. They soon pick up on you doing the dishes for your woman, while missing the rugby on TV! They admire it and eventually they will emulate it. When they are ready.

There is then permanent value in this, as it is based on choice!

Telling them to "do the bloody dishes once in a while" is not ever going to achieve such virtue or any free and happy choice to help. Just set the example in your own life, your own actions and trust that the good in your child will respect that and want to learn from it!

Naturally, if you don't make your parenting a "bloody hard job" by driving your kids up the walls with it, you later never have to complain about how "hard it was to raise children," the saddest of all things to hear from a parent!

Programming is child-abuse, clearly, and does not work with smart kids.

The only thing that works in parenting is to use your hammer well, to cook food joyfully and to clean the house with a song! Then a kid will copy your attitude and not see house-skills as a necessary evil and as despised "work." And then you don't need any discipline, commands, naggings and lectures, which only serve to alienate your child anyway.

It is astonishing to the western mind to observe how untouched tribal people in the rainforest never raise their voices towards children, never scold or punish and always talk respectfully to them! The effect is that boys and girls see it as a great honor to be entrusted with a task or responsibility to help the family. You never see a child reluctant to help or uninterested in learning in such villages. Those kids take tremendous pride in helping and do not expect any further reward.

It is possible to cultivate just such a state of socially intact, bright-eyed cooperation in your own child by playing chess! Try playing when your daughter asks you for it, play well, and make the game of chess an instrument for cultivating respect!

Say thank you for the game after you won! Mention what you might have learned.

Mention the best move your daughter made and how smart that was. And be done.

Enjoy your life with a teenager when most parents struggle!

Chapter 9: Control and Trust

It begins when the pregnancy test shows positive. Suddenly the expectant mother should not eat this and not that and not smoke, not drink any alcohol, not work much, just rest, smile and eat folic acid. Rules! Loss of freedom! And a new father who wants her to do all things just right...

The expectant dad, trying to control the alcohol and nicotine intake of the mother is, as life shows, on collision course with human nature, and much better off putting his faith in trusting the mother. Most of the time...

The control-freak dad not eliminated here, usually gets sick during birth or is not wanted there by the mother.

I was so gaga by just holding Mana, my firstborn daughter, in my arms, stunned by her incredible vulnerability and helplessness, that I became the instant super-hero protector for this little girl! The smell of her warm scalp and neck alone enslaved me as her protector for life, and her safety became my very highest priority.

It took her eighteen months to sort me out:

We lived in a two-story house on high stilts by the river, which had very steep, high steps to the first floor and again inside to the second story. All straight as, in stark evidence of my humble carpentry skills! These stairs absolutely fascinated Mana at the peak of her crawling career and she would get there as fast as a coin can drop...

Building rails and doors being awkward and too expensive, I used large pot-plants and heavy planters to block the outside stairs, and cardboard boxes to block the lower steps inside. I did my damnedest to prevent a fall, which to my mind had to be fatal for sure. Especially Mana's sweetest compulsion—approaching the outdoor steps in daddy's large gumboots—had me far too worried to drop my control.

And yet—one day, Mana monkey-climbed over the planter and rolled down the outside stairs helter-skelter, head over heels, shaking the entire house and my entire sense of control! She then landed like a cat in the grass, quite happy and unhurt, her curiosity satisfied—her dad a tachycardic wreck!

The same advanced monkey-techniques naturally got her exploring the sensation of shooting down the inside stairs as well, after cleverly getting past the blockage of piled-up cardboard boxes! She hit the floor head-first in a big, house-shaking bang and I would for years inspect her head-shape after unusual or silly comments...

From then on, I lived with Murphy's Law and in awe of the hardness of Mana's head—and the "vulnerable little thing" knew it...

My last great "test" was when she fell backward through a false wall in Ubud, Bali, at nineteen months old. She fell five meters deep onto slanting concrete and I thought this is it and prepared for imminent heart-attack. But she was so good by then at falling, that again she had landed like a kitten, smiling sweetly when I picked her up.

In summary, I could firmly trust Mana to outwit all my controlling measures to prevent the things I was most scared of...I gave up the idea of control and perfect safety soon after this and replaced it with trust. I let go of fear. Or rather—Mana knocked it out of me! And never had an accident again...

We all do, individually and collectively, consciously or subliminally, utterly believe in control. We believe that uncontrolled, unregulated or uncivilized humans must surely be chaotic, selfish and barbaric. We believe that our children need imposed discipline, regulation and parental control, or they would become or remain wild, without character and unshaped.

We believe these things with religious conviction, although their application never works, and despite all the evidence to the contrary!

A two-year old is trying to show us that already in what we call the "terrible two" or whatever we label it off as, when she simply and powerfully says—NO!—to everything imposed on her without her consent.

And the "rebellious" teenager then just wants that one thing—to destroy your control over her! The son's slaying of the father along the patterns of Oedipus is necessary to walk one's own path and out of father's shadow! But parents never see that before their control is in tatters...

Politicians similarly don't recognize that to control (= incarcerate, kill, punish) the criminal does not affect the causes or the existence of crime any more than killing soldiers can end any conflicts.

The "best minds" in what they call "Intelligence" today suggest, as in the most barbaric times, that to "eliminate" the terrorist (= freedom fighter) and to torture any suspects, and to bomb civilians, will "end the terrorist threat!"

They do not perceive that their own use of violence *celebrates* the "terrorist's" violent means as perfectly legitimate! Their thinking is—look, we too can't think of alternatives to violence to get our views respected. We use those same methods and just hit back a hundred times harder! Law of the fist for the righteous!

Can we really not perceive how we breed millions of new young "terrorists" among kids whose parents, homes, relatives or friends, have been torn to pieces by our democratic bombs? And amongst those who worship the bomber pilots as heroes? No, we most certainly do not have that much intelligence.

As parents, to simply lock up people or shoot them when we see them breaking our rules is not going to work particularly well. It does not work, whether you ask an honest prison warden, or a stat chart, or a sensible parent or a police officer. Control leads only to more prisons, more heavily armed police, to more "tiger-moms" and to more screwed up, angry kids.

Not to speak of everlasting war with the rest of the world...

And with all our friends, our children, our partners!

And do you really believe *you* are in control of *your* life?

Do you think Bobby Fisher can control what happens on the chess-board?

Certainly, we do need to make a few rules for life and chess. And there usually is some punishment for breaking those rules, which is only natural. If, for instance, you don't consider what the other guy plans, you see only half of the truth and it may lose you the queen or the respect of others. But is it necessary for a parent to invent additional rules and sanctions in order to manipulate a child into fundamental obedience?

Instead of mutually agreeing on rules, as in chess, we first make people hate the rules we make up and then keep punishing them. We say— "I don't care if he hates the rule, as long as he sticks to it..."

Of course, this is experienced as disrespectful control by the free citizen, by the child, the partner...and—big surprise! —it creates rebellion!

Our total control wish is not only not working, but it is the original cause that creates all resistance and all "rebellious teenagers." To acknowledge this goes in the face of our culture, our collective misconceptions and of the democratic majority—which is why we have wars and "wayward" teenagers...

It requires great personal strength to conjure up the courage to look where our belief in over-control comes from. That it is unadmitted fear! That fear arises even more after we strike fear into others.

The more violent we are as a society (to animals, to other societies and to children mostly), the more violence we can of course expect back, which constantly increases our latent fear.

We even fear ourselves and what we might do if we "lose control" ...and this is because we don't really know ourselves, only those identifications, names and cultural programs we keep playing out...

We ourselves have never lived in a culture of self-development, of truth, or of respectful, peaceful self-responsibility!

As parents, we fear our kids might become as "bad" as we suspect ourselves to be, and we'll do all to prevent that, thereby creating a monstrous double standard.

Only the slightly more afflicted parents are sometimes recognized as control-freaks by the rest—but our kids *all* recognize their parents in that capacity!

There is of course nothing wrong with having control when driving a car or when playing chess or when telling a kid to get dressed. Control becomes wrong and dangerous however, when we sit tense and scared in a car, watching other cars like a constant death-threat. It becomes wrong when a chess-player acts from fear of losing, or from a sense of self-importance, and when he can't enjoy his mistakes.

And it is wrong where a parent replaces trust with control!

In chess, we don't know what move our opponent is going to make. We can't control that at all! Just as we can't control the actions of our child!

We can only control our own actions. We can try to get right what we have a right to control—our own choices and actions. Not other people's choices and actions!!

This we can very easily learn from chess, and that is when we begin having some actual control on the board—and also as a parent who then simply gets his own moves right.

We can either understand this in time—or we will lose our children in their teenage years, when any attempt to control them is thrown back into our solemn faces by a new-born freedom fighter...

To break parental control is to a teenager absolutely necessary! How else would a girl ever be able to leave her beloved father's home and move in with a lover she barely knows? How would a boy arise from his father's shadow and follow his own rule and sense? Evolution would go in circles of repetitive and sterile traditions...

Only trust can bring any solution here! Trust that your kid can look after herself, learn from experience and make her own moves in life! Trust in the universe as a safe place!

Trust in your own ability to let go...

Show this trust to your kid to foster self-responsibility!

Don't stay under the tree your child climbs, trying to catch it! Walk away trusting she will not fall or fall well!

When she brings home the fat, ugly, hairy boyfriend—trust that she knows better than you do what she needs at that time from that person.

Trust that you yourself know very little, or else she will tell you so.

It is true to some degree that the more we love our kids, the more we worry. But reality isn't as prescriptive or condemning as that and leaves us a way out of eternal worries. The name of this path is trust, and this trust is, as it always includes respect, the principal key to enlightened parenting!

But we throw around words like trust or love or freedom today and each one of us understands a different thing by the same word. So, let us be clear about what trust really means beyond the many versions of our shared illusion:

Having trust in our child must not mean to trust that she will fulfill our expectations punctually, embrace our vision for her future, or that she will turn out 'just right' by being always obedient!

It is not trust to always believe a toddler safe beside a pool or a stairway, or to just suppose he will naturally always get it right as long as we don't interfere. That would be conceptual philosophy, not the practical, observant path we are looking at here.

We cannot replace acute awareness with disengagement or define trust as blind faith.

No, trust is not casually or easily acquired, or simply adopted as a new favorite attitude. It is gradually attained and occurs in its pure form only rather rarely.

Wise men trust nobody, just like the wild deer doesn't. That is the authentic natural state. What we commonly call trust is simply predictability! We trust the lights turn from red to green. We trust our wives not to be attracted to other men. We trust the sun will rise in the morning. This is all faith in predictability only—a purely empirical response based on yesterday's facts.

True trust is much more than that...

It always starts with yourself, naturally!

The question of whether you are going to be trusted by your children in the future and are able to trust them in return, firstly depends on whether you trust yourself.

What do you trust about yourself? That you are loyal, honest, respectful, honorable?

Do you trust yourself when drunk? When driving? When scared? When angry?

This can be a rather deep and difficult meditation, but you need this time to know exactly to what level you can trust yourself. Never expect others to trust you more than you trust yourself, including your children, or you will feel like a hypocrite, and rightly so!

How then can you develop trust in yourself, in your actions, in your clarity of mind and good sense of judgment? —Play chess and meditate on the "next true move!"

By aiming to get the next move "just right" on the chess-board our mind shifts into a state of being solely responsible and acutely committed. You look at everything, at all possibilities and at all combinations. Even from bizarre angles. Even at the perception from your opponent's perspective! At things that might go wrong. At the future!

And then, only when you are quite content of having diligently performed the act of complete observation, when you know you have done your best—then you act decisively and make your move! With a steady hand.

Soon you will know that you can trust your decisions! Now, after a few weeks of playing like this, you can be trusted by others simply because you can trust yourself! Trust yourself to be a rational, reasonable, observant, well-balanced, caring and capable person, right? And once you have these qualities yourself—you won't need your kid to acquire them *for you*! You actually become an example by living up to your own self.

Now you are ready to have a child that looks up at you with large eyes full of absolute trust, a trust you must now daily earn and confirm, and keep sacred without ever betraying it...

You can't lie on the chess-board and you must not lie to your children, ever!

Then you are worthy of their trust.

By having trust in yourself—you can live up to their trust.

It was easy to trust my girls with the river after teaching them to swim and climb out by themselves. I also trusted them with the big black dog, after recognizing their skill and gentleness and that of the dog. I trusted them to solo-drive the car and to go out until they were ready to come home, at age twelve. They were simply competent enough, and not just because of their black-belts, but because of their ability to read situations and people correctly.

I trusted them to be fast-learning creatures in a wilderness I could never hope to control, to be creatures responsible for themselves and for their environment, capable of looking after themselves and others.

To see Mana at age three with her baby-sister, a perfect little mother, made my heart ache with respect, love and trust every minute of every day.

When Morgana was born, I had mostly overcome my anxious protector-trip and allowed them both to find their own boundaries. After a great pregnancy, Morgana did a complete push-up on the day of her birth, holding her head straight forward like a turtle, and she went for her first baby-swim in the river the day after.

She later joined our karate-club at an unprecedented eighteen months of age, together with her four-year-old sister, after demonstrating the necessary discipline and attention-span to convince the sensei who saw five as the minimum age.

I watched my girls in hundreds of dojo- and tournament fights and I took them for three-day walks through rainforest, let them ride camels, dogs, horses, elephants, giant tortoises and sheep, and generally experience all those "dangerous" things that parents call "don't touch," like snakes, spiders, knives or big dogs.

At age five, they were both able and happy to cook up a good variety of decent meals, do the dishes without breaking a plate, and clean up their room without being told. (Although at fifteen they both graduated to allowing chaos back into their rooms, of course...)

My growing trust and genuine respect paid daily dividends when considering their high levels of self-mastery, competence and confidence, and my own stress-free life.

Trust created competence and competence created more trust...

They had acquired massive self-discipline from always being guided by their own experience and volition, rather than through being "disciplined" by a parent. I did never worry therefore when they were off to some party, about what terrible thing they might do when I wasn't there...

They had allowed me, the super-hero control freak, to drop all my fear-driven control and had replaced it with real trust!

It is for this reason that parenting for me was only ever the purest pleasure, the greatest of pleasures and—an immense honor.

And best of all—it really helped me grow up.

Chapter 10: Competence and Confidence

Beginners at chess will naturally lack great confidence because they have as yet little competence. There is no point in "boosting" their confidence at this stage, as this would make them throw their queen forward like a flaming sword and lose it every time, until their confidence adjusts to reality. Actual confidence however is simply the direct result of actual competence!

Confidence that exceeds competence is called foolishness, which is what you get when taking a self-assertiveness course or if you have been raised by a praise-all-you-can parent. Artificial confidence never lasts and is exceedingly dangerous!

Once a kid has clearly learned how to check-mate a bare king with only a rook and has practiced this successfully against various players, this kid will be absolutely confident to do this at any time against any player, even a grandmaster!

Eventually, this kid needs only glance at a position to know who is going to win and what the right move is—and has by then acquired such competence that he generally trusts himself to see all kind of problems presented and find the appropriate solution, even for other players or in other fields.

To acquire competence is the only way how confidence naturally develops and how it keeps its balance!

Children do not become confident through praise and parental assertions of how smart and how pretty they are! They will always feel just as truly confident as they feel competent at what matters to them, and that is their balance, their safety!

Of course, "confidence" has also much to do with approval by the peer-group, with whether a kid is considered popular and cool. But what makes a kid "cool" is nothing but competence! A boy, who is competent at soccer or base-ball, and competent at making friends with pretty girls, is thus "cool" and popular.

A girl, competent at attracting boys, at knowing how to dress and how to work her face-book, and who can talk and listen, and who is an ice-dancer, will be popular and "cool" to her friends.

Parents who "raise" their kids to obedience instead and to a so-called "competence" of their own narrow definition will inevitably fail to let their children make their own choice in experience and challenge. Such a kid cannot learn competence from sneaking out at night, having an amazing adventure with friends and then not getting caught or hit by any fall-out! An always obedient boy never gets into a fight, never learns to protect himself and never earns anybody's respect, much less his own.

In our day, in western society, not in principle, it is mostly the girls who desperately lack confidence. This is because being told "you are nice and pretty" isn't exactly the path to competence and being protected from all "hurt" and risk as a little kid does not help either.

My girls did chess, karate, horse-riding and a lot of travel on shoestring, which are the four best methods for developing competence I could think of, apart from skilled work like cooking or pruning trees. I always tried my best not to "rescue" them or "help" before they had completed a task; but afterwards, I would ask their advice or opinion on those matters they had been working on. This is the soil on which competence grows!

It was not always easy. To watch Morgana fight big Maori girls twice her size in tournaments was initially gut-wrenching. But she loved it and excelled at it and gained confidence from it for all other areas of her life.

Until one day I coaxed from a rather quiet Morgana that five Maori-girls at school had promised her the "bash." I knew from experience that "Kerikeri High" had no working policy for bullies and took no functional steps to protect a prospective victim. So, I told her to take the speaker of the group down hard and fast, if she ever got cornered by a gang, assuring her that nobody would likely follow the example of that leader...

Next day she came home rather cheerful, after having been ambushed outside school by seven big, strapping Maori chicks, and challenged to fight so as to prove the worth of her black belt. She had given the biggest girl two good shots to the head, after which she and her mates had had enough and—they all proceeded to making friends!

In fact, most girls wanted to be friends with Morgana after this and nobody else without a belt ever challenged her to fight again. She became very popular and pretty much the epitome of "cool," keeping a good check on bullies.

This is where I fully understood that competence and confidence are the two sides of one and the same coin, and I began to really enjoy the fruit of my earlier struggles about letting them take risks and face hardships.

Many girls experience a sudden loss of confidence when they reach puberty. Again, the reason for this is a sudden recognition of incompetence, now incompetence about being or becoming a woman. Without any rites of passage whatsoever, a girl's coming of age in western society is a blind stumble into a supposed womanhood that must not be explored before it is too late, and for which there are few competent and admired examples beyond "Women's Weekly!"

Sex, described as the root of all disease and unwanted children, is widely viewed as morally wrong and as devoid of goodness and worth. This leads to feelings of guilt, self-reproach, to parental and later self-condemnation. Is it a wonder then, that she dislikes her own body, this new instrument of sexual frustration, sees it as animalistic and as too womanly (= too fat)?

Very few western women like their bodies at that age, or any body-hair reminding them of their sexuality, far less than ten per cent.

Many never catch up on womanly competence, relying on the supposed virtue of time passing...

For a solo-father to counter-act this cultural incompetence in matters of sex and the sexual incompetence this causes in girls, all by himself, is pretty much impossible. What girls need at this age is a sexually competent, mature woman who can teach them the example of being a proud, developed female.

The sole father should try and help spot such a woman (God, did I try...), and must not feel jealous when a woman chosen by his daughter becomes temporarily more important than he is.

For a sole parent to be fully competent means to include all (competent) available help with open gratitude, rather than to rely solely on one's own genius...

Clear signs of deficient womanly confidence are the plucking of eye-brows to a line and the shaving of legs, as well as other extermination-warfare against body-hair. This behavior shows clearly that dependence on fashionable opinion has outweighed self-acceptance as a human animal and as a sexual female.

There is no profit in trying to "stop" these self-mutilations, once they start seeing their bodies as the *other* self and their womanhood as something derived from peer-acceptance.

Only a good and powerful womanly example could at this late stage remind the young girl of the competence she really seeks.

Most girls never dare to stand up against popular opinion in their group and hate to be found "different" in any way. Girls with intact eye-brows thus get attacked as "dogs," or "hillbillies," and usually can't stand on their own feet enough to handle this kind of pressure.

I found that karate helps with maintaining useable fingernails, chess with reliance on their own judgment, and travel with the recognition of the arbitrariness of cultural definitions. A paternal attitude of respect for women naturally helps with self-acceptance and self-discovery. But I wanted them to expand their existing competence to all areas in life.

My solution here was to travel! I soon found they were fully competent riding elephants along the Thai/Burmese border, even when the elephant rolled in a river to cool itself or walked briskly downhill!

They were able to convert currencies and prices in their heads, able to communicate with Cambodian, or Lao, or non-English-speaking tribal Lisu or Lahu people; they were running fearless, but wise of snakes, they learned to spot con-men and pick-pockets and saw the world through many different perspectives throughout our four-month trips.

Attracted by the Pinoy heart-power, we spent much intense time on Negros and other islands in the Philippines, where the local, even the urban people set such a standard of gentle lovingness, of lie-free openness, of incredible motherliness and depth of social interaction—that the world-view of the experiencing child is wonderfully and magically expanded by a richness of heart, a note of trust in the universe and in general goodness.

The tribal Bukidnon are another world again, where the children face a set of challenges that to a courageous white kid offer quick development of quite unrecognized parts of the human potential and lift her out of her cultural "box" and all those fixed facts, like taking meals for granted.

The Philippines are like one big kindergarten! Everybody loves your child, particularly if she is blond and outgoing, interested and energetic. You can trust your environment, because the very rare odd-ball posing a possible threat will be known, seen and controlled by hundreds of caring and observing and responsible Pinoys—and that odd guy knows it!

They learn how to open and drink a coconut, how to weave a wall or a roof from Nipa-leaves, they climb up the coconut tree for Tuba (fermented nectar), they hunt iguana with a bolo (machete) and split bamboo with it for furniture. They get to hold a hundred babies a day and to stand in groups of only females, laughing and chatting and laughing until they fall all over each other and stay friends for ever...

They get to sail a boat, to swim and dive like fish among the countless colors of other fish, along white sand beaches, blue sky and wooded mountains. They learn what a completely open and profoundly "good" face looks like in an old tribal man and what happiness can be in an emotionally healthy child.

They are not prevented, but will experience women giving birth in a birth-house or their nipa-hut—as a wonderful, positive, chemical-smell-free event that isn't scary...

They see old people die.

They put their faces deep into a sun-warm, summer-ripe mango and have another five when they so choose.

They get to know and copy the respectful relationship their local friends have with their elders and family, while living within that family.

I saw such things as empathy, true social ability and warmth of heart, generosity, humility and motherliness, qualities that we all wish for in our prisoners and in our criminals, and for our young children hopefully—grow on my girls inside weeks, in such a natural and easily integrated way that everybody felt they were competent little jungle-kids and as capable as the Filipino children they ran with, at catching a fish, at getting the local price at the market or at being responsible for a few smaller kids.

By "doing" very little directly to "raise" my daughters in such places, I instead invited the world and nature herself to help, and I trusted in that. I trusted that being around heaps of very open women, who fully demonstrate without deception what being a female really is and what it can mean to be a mother—my girls would absorb what their souls needed, without further philosophy from me.

It worked, of course.

Any lack of confidence is terribly un-cool in the western world as it always signals a lack of competence to others. Those who get left behind here, make up most of those teenage suicides that we cannot explain at all!

An approach to "fix" the insecure teenager with "counseling" or such can never work.

In order to develop the competence needed to face who we are and to know where we want to go, and how and why—we need to begin early! As small children!

If we are allowed to play with the dog, to fall in the pool, to get stuck in mud, to run with tribal kids, to hunt and fish and to hurt and heal ourselves—only then do we become competent!

If we obediently sit by the table, properly dressed, and agree always with what daddy says—we become incompetent!

The good news is that Nature gets it far more often right than the most skillful parent. It is therefore a good idea not to think of yourself as too "competent!" Employ instead your competence by always knowing when to leave things alone and when to trust your kids...

What should you do if your three-year-old baby-girl runs into a meadow full of flowers and bees? Stop her? Frighten her with warnings?

I suggest you leave her to it for a while. Then possibly join and point out the bees as good little fellows that make honey and fruit. "How can such little things protect themselves and their honey? By having a sting! Cool, aye? But if you step on them or scare them, they automatically sting you, without even wanting it. Then they die. So be careful. And if you get stung, come or call and we put vinegar over it..."

After this you never warn about bees again!

Your girl learns that bees have a sting.

She also learns that warnings even given only once are worth remembering.

She learns to be prepared about getting stung. And will get stung! Hopefully!

And she learns that this is no reason to avoid the pretty meadow!!

And she learns how to act and deal with the eventuality of a sting.

When she does get stung, you tell her how good that is for rheumatism and for immunity and how she gets much stronger now. Tell her to be grateful to the bee for that.

You also show her ribwort plantain, in case there is no vinegar, to ease the momentary burn and to empower her self-healing.

But for love's sake—don't interfere with her self-motivated walk into the meadow over a few bees!

If you can't do that—work on your own confidence!

Start with your own competence as a person!

Are you a good example for developing your hidden skills?

Why not play another painful game against that guy who always beats you?

Be truthful with yourself here, so that you can also always be truthful to your kids.

Respect your own self and your own abilities first—so that you will not talk down to your children, not even to the baby...

Expect yourself to become more and more competent and respect yourself for that!

It is very important to always answer your children's questions honestly and competently and—to leave the question alive!

You will find that once you master your own self, there is no need at all to master your kids or to resort to disciplinary measures or artificial praise.

Work on your own competence and then allow your kids to naturally follow your and Nature's examples to earn their own competence!

Then you and your kids can be confident about life and successful at a real education that encompasses the soul, social and emotional intelligence, basic life-skills and the sheer joy of learning.

Chapter 11: Tactical moves

"Dad, can I watch 'Outrageous Fortune' now?" She looks at dad but takes no answer for granted. Dad's strategic position is based on true respect underlying a genuinely asked question. From such a position, he can afford a few tactical moves which would be quite futile to attempt from a weaker, merely authority-based position.

He can suggest alternatives!

The important thing is that dad does not act or speak from an automated or semi-aware state of mind! He needs to recognize this little, arbitrary moment as an opportunity for tactical parenting, instead of allowing parenting to become confined to nagging-sessions or the conveyance of moralistic dogma. Parenting is always here now and only the parent conscious of this will be successful with his tactical moves, which are simply moves he is highly conscious of.

The parent needs to be aware of the larger picture, of course. Dad might ask "how did the job pruning the feijoa trees go? All good?" Or "I thought we might go fishing?"

Had his daughter asked to watch "Simpsons," then he definitely needs to make a better suggestion! To watch "Simpsons" is no reward and no true joy! TV is never a reward and the tactical parent prevents any such notion from developing! He would instead suggest taking time for a game of chess or badminton, whatever beats Simpsons.

With "Outrageous Fortune" it's a little different. This is good cultural stuff and out of the box fun, and mom might say "sure, and so will I. If we get the kitchen cleaned up by then..."

It does not matter so much what you decide. What matters is to be free rather than automated, aware rather than half-asleep to the opportunities and moments that amount to parenting. Don't just "limit" or "control" TV or internet use; it only makes it far more interesting! Instead point out the idiocies and show some contempt for filling one's mind and time with cheap entertainment and commercial operators' suggestions of what is reality! Offer games, sport and natural observation as more attractive alternatives! After you have given your best in guidance—withdraw respectfully to let your kid decide and make her choices!

The biggest reason why kids watch TV is having nothing better to do! Just like there are only street-kids when there is nothing better to do! To say "no" to TV does not work. Your kid will watch it at friend's places or move out from home early and buy a TV! Forbidding a thing just makes it more attractive. Be real about this and replace control with better moves that convince your kid that there is indeed much cooler stuff out there than TV. To be against TV is not to master it. The power of advertising, which brainwashes all TV kids into becoming stupid, gullible consumers, is not avoided by paying it no attention. It seeps into their subconscious minds unfiltered, unless you undo the manipulation while it happens! Teach your kid to recognize all the "tricks" ads use to make her do and buy things she does not really want! Show how to discern the target group, the false promises and the outright lies, until she is too conscious of those intentions to just let them all in, undigested, unchecked, unverified! Encourage spotting the illusions! This makes for a good game!

One can, as a family, pick those treasures TV also has to offer, like the "Crocodile Hunter" Steve Irving, or David Attenborough, Jamie Oliver, and other programs that derive from real teachers of our time and awaken interest beyond the usual politically correct nonsense. Some programs are valuable if shared responsibly as a family.

If you'd rather have him do some educational homework, ask your kid what value he gets out of a film; ask him to tell you the gist or the full length of a movie, depending on what lesson is offering itself—English, or history, or geography, or archeology...

What move then do you make when your daughter "withdraws" into the internet at age twelve, when you only know her from passing food through a hesitantly opened door...?

Well, then you need to recognize that the limited mental world of internet is still giving your daughter more interactivity and more possibilities than the world *you* are offering her!

Offer something better consistently—and she won't fall in love with the deprivation of senses her computer is exposing her to...

Should you censure the things your son is allowed to watch? Forget it! This does not work. If he really wants to watch pornography, he will, if he has any brains—by which time nudity has become something "bad," secret and underground...and *you* have forced him to that!

Suppressing sexual interest leads to sociopathic curiosity, not to sainthood!

Let him watch what he wants, but stay with him in this new world, explore together and share what you both think respectfully. What he wants, is to see a large variety of naked woman and clearly visible vagina! What could possibly be wrong with wanting that and with getting it? Guide him along and hint at the crudeness of reduction, but also listen to what *he* sees as "good" or "bad" pictures and watch on what interests he lingers. Don't judge that! You'll get to know your own kid much better, you can practice your own honesty this way and—you learn to trust your son and your daughter, because you know you can trust them! You're on their side, so—they trust you too.

Trust her to make the right choices for *her*! Then you can withdraw. Don't hover. Just listen to her with more heart than Face-book and introduce living, physical interactive possibilities to your child's life that she will much prefer to a purely mental world.

It has to be clear to any even half-baked parent, that to leave a toddler or young kid watching TV alone for any length of time, is utterly irresponsible, as it will determine your kid's world view and make him addicted to being programmed and conditioned by others.

As in chess, a parent should consider all possible moves and make choices based on respect, honesty and potential.

So, what would you do if your daughter wants to go to a party where you suspect drug use or frivolous boys? If you just say "no" to it, you can be sure that your "little girl" will seek such experiences as soon as you don't look, and she will then never tell you about it.

You can also be certain that she never learns how to say an authentic "no" from inside herself, to indiscriminate use of drugs or to boys with nothing but incompetent sex on their little minds!

To even use the word "drugs" creates a choice-less ignorance that will equate a natural healing-herb with dangerous chemicals that can quickly destroy her life. Sit down instead and discuss the dangers for what they really are! Acknowledge and respect your daughter's desire to make out-of-the-box experiences and consider together how they can be safely and sensibly made or other alternatives found.

If you tell your daughter that marijuana and sex before marriage are of the devil—you will lose her trust and her respect for your competence! She will thereafter assume incompetence in whatever you say and think that amphetamines or heroin or prostitution are just as fine as those natural herbs, and she will probably engage in secret, unprotected and disappointing sexual activities and drug use, just as all her (always more competent!) friends do! Demands and punishments do not change this fact and once you have made that move you cannot take it back...

The tactical move is to inform yourself properly, to explain sex as a divine art, a sacred union and as based on self-respect! Teach the difference between chemicals and shamanic herbs! Stay on your teenager's side!

It never works to teach to say "no." What works is honesty—followed by trust!

Even as a solo-dad, I never once warned my girls off sex. I told them how wonderful sex can be with the right partner, if they know what they are doing and if they respect their emotional reality and biological safety. I never had awkward feelings talking about sex, nor did I ever talk down to them as recipients of my abundant wisdom. We discussed sex much like we discussed positions on the chess-board. I trusted their intelligence and self-responsibility not to get into "bad" situations or accidental pregnancies, and so they never did. They are now open with their boy-friends and experiences and about how they feel about difficult emotional decisions.

A sex education based on saying "no," on the threat of STDs, unwanted pregnancy and date-rape, is in its selective negativity simply not credible and thus cannot work! All kids recognize this as fear-driven parental control and discard it as such in the face of wonder...

Sex education needs to confirm sex as a most special, divine gift that must not be wrongly used! The tactical move here is to be a source of interesting information, rather than the stalwart defender of religious or cultural dogma!

Your kid needs to trust you as competent, as standing by her side—or she will stop hearing you, just to preserve a modicum of goodness about how she feels!

So, let your daughter go to the party of her choice, when she is fifteen, if you trust her, and prepare her for the challenges she faces without conditioning her views. Explain to her how boys may think and what they might try—but without making them wrong!

Your chess-kid knows from experience what happens to a lonely queen that goes for half-cooked solo-adventures without staying connected to the other pieces, like friends and parents. She knows that impulse alone is only going to get the queen trapped, no matter how smart she is. You too need to trust that and express that trust!

Competence and trust are the only working basis in all areas of child-raising and the only thing that keeps your teenager from disengaging.

Parents who rely on their "authority," on their "love," financial power, and on control will always fail and end up losing all control, all authority, and the power to guide their teenager. We all know this without often admitting it...

To be tactical must not mean to manipulate! It means nurturing good choices in a child by allowing her to be self-responsible to the highest degree.

"But be home by eleven pm" —takes away all self-determination. Such a kid will look at the clock, rather than at how she feels inside or at how much she is enjoying herself. She will stay till eleven, even if she's had enough at ten, and she will interrupt a really important conversation she had just to be obedient. She will then resent this and she will not be able to learn making decisions based on how things develop. Nothing could be more un-tactical than such attempts at control.

A kid needs to be aware of how you feel, certainly, and may be call you if she decides to stay longer, but this has to arise from her own connectedness (to the other pieces) and from true respect, not from a demand, if it is to become a part of who she is.

Your teenager is indeed quite capable of feeling out risk, feeling a boy's intentions, and feeling the fear of what some drug may do. She simply often lacks the self-assurance to assess it all quickly enough. A lack of self-esteem may sway her towards accepting those notions accepted by her friends and override those subtler intuitive warnings she has no practice in heeding.

The worst thing a parent can therefore do is to make a kid or teenager "wrong" about how she sees the world! This always takes a heavy toll on self-worth and self-reliance.

But neither should a smaller child get "encouraged" every time she shows you a picture!

This patronizing behavior is experienced by your kid as—disinterest, contempt, incompetence and dishonesty. She learns from this example to become patronizing towards you, too, and will act disinterested, become untruthful and incompetent. And then you wonder where in hell she got it from, since your intentions were all "nurturing," "supportive" and "positive…"

The truth is that perpetual nurturing creates kids who can't feed themselves! That "support" often creates mentally crippled, incompetent children who can't take critique and give up in the face of every little hardship!

These very common mistakes are all self-defeating moves leading to the stale-mate of ineffective parenting.

If your child shows you her paintings, what should you do?

Firstly, take a genuine interest if you can! Look at what there really is. Don't judge.

Say what you see. Be honest about it, be truly open to it. Maybe you see something "funny" or well-executed, clear of message, or else—superficial, uncommitted, unfinished. You can say all that. After you have looked, really looked, with respect!

Only if you can recognize a careless "test-picture" as such and give it minimal attention, will you keep your child's respect and get truly amazing paintings. Your child learns that you can see the difference. That you bother to look…

This is where chess is such a fantastic medium. Sometimes your off-shoot plays hurriedly or with a lack of commitment, and you will both say afterwards that it wasn't so good. But then there are games or combinations of moves that just stand out, that are brilliant. And here you need enough joy or passion to cry out loud over the genius your youngster has just demonstrated! Now you can show some genuine pride that will be received as true encouragement and much valued by your son or daughter!

As one more example for what I mean by "tactical moves" may serve how to teach your kid to say "thank you" after a game, or when given a present.

If you always expect your kid to say "thank you," whatever she is offered, then the development of actual gratitude becomes impossible! Gratitude is supposed to be a real, genuine feeling, may be the most precious of all feelings, and it needs to be cultivated in the heart, not as an empty, formal gesture that is not felt and only supposed to shine a good light on the parents' ability to instill "manners." Kids expected to say thank you like a robot cannot possibly develop a true sense of gratitude, nor do they learn that some things should not be accepted at all...

The best tactical move is not to expect the well-mannered formal response, but to show by example how you can be truly grateful yourself and how that feels to others!

The kid who always gets what she wants can of course never develop gratitude and neither can you as long as you expect your kid to always do what you want!

Keep in mind that, as in chess, tactical moves can only work if your strategic position allows for them, if you got your own pieces in the right place at the right time and if you are not too full of yourself to drop the original plan you concocted before the game was even on and all the players had their say.

Chapter 12: Rules and their breaking

In chess, we willingly learn to obey the rules. These are rules that make sense to us and that we can accept without conflict. A rook can only move along straight lines—this rule, although quite arbitrary, is easily respected! If you want to play chess that is...

The player has no issue with respecting those basic rules, which are much like laws of nature. There is wind—live with it! It can rain water—accept that and you can still play!

Only if we accept all the rules of the game—are we players.

A kid who learns and accepts those rules willingly, happily, gratefully—and then sticks by them all, entirely by her own decision and inner drive—never needs to be scolded, reminded of the rules or disciplined! She is already happily learning self-discipline and self-responsibility with every move she makes!

And it is his *own* triumph and her *own* path—not our authoritarian attempt to program ideas of "discipline" into their humiliated minds...

Certainly, this is true for any sport or for music and we are seeing it every day in how "stars" are born, not from schooling, but from sports and singing, which is from the physical body and from the heart. Our minds remain well outside of "stardom" where schools do not enable self-responsibility, choice and self-development in children—where they suffocate it by relying on authority and on force.

When a child is disciplined to obey unaccepted rules and to learn unasked-for answers from an un-chosen teacher who demands respect before he earns it—she cannot possibly learn self-respect, respect, self-discipline or a love for learning as such! Those kids then know they are at school because they have to, not by choice, and naturally they often "hate" or at least disrespect their teacher. As you would, too, if forced into a room with an appointed preacher who is paid to feed you what somebody, somewhere up there, considers worthwhile information at this particular time and to all present! You think this can develop intelligence?? It stifles every spark of it that could burn beyond copy-cat learning and trying to please the teacher! The smart kid will likely look out of the window and listen to the birds...

Or she won't question being taught a subject of no interest to her in the future... She then gets used to not being asked, to not being respected. To be called "stupid" or a "dreamer," or directly told (as schools will!) "not to get smart" and not to "talk back." This is what we do to our kids in schools—we devalue the idea of "teacher" to mean nothing more than "indoctrinator" and "administrator," a tool of the state and of economic and social requirements, who feeds all those "facts" into young brains that are needed to run those already existing machines of manufacturing. Thus, we produce well-programmed citizens who do not challenge authority or the status quo. That is what schools do. This is the rule.

A school, or teacher, with anything like what we misname as "common sense" would soon realize, to give a typical example, that learning happens via the *senses*! All of our senses, not just two, naturally! At school, we learn only by looking(reading) and by listening(instructions), whereas real learning includes tasting, smelling, and touching, just as it naturally happens outside of school. It also includes intuiting, which is what we may count as the "six's sense," or simply understood as the wisdom present in the body, its cells, its DNA; the subliminal inner sense. For the weirdest reasons, our culture does not recognize any sense apart from the auditory and the visual sense as necessary for effective and balanced learning!! In fact, modern man has just about lost his sense of smell entirely through unbalanced learning, or at least equates "smell" with negative or "bad" smell, and thus deems it an "inappropriate" subject of learning. It is us, the parents, the teachers, the culturally completely brainwashed adults, who have lost most of our senses to lack of attention! We ourselves were "schooled" to see and hear, but not to feel, smell, taste or touch, which makes our teachings and our example in principle counterproductive, damaging, limiting. We have mostly lost at least four of our senses, and our schooling or parenting is thus always about "don't touch," "don't fart," "don't eat" during class, and about ignoring how any kid really feels and perceives. Even what kids can learn using only two senses will be distorted and devalued by the isolation and disconnection of two-dimensional learning. Children are becoming worse and worse as listeners, and what they mostly see are the omnipresent images of consumerism and violence and computer screens. With the fine exception of Rudolf Steiner Schools, the sense of touch has been utterly ignored in classrooms where holding a pen is the peak of finger-skill development. And our sense of taste has deteriorated in a consumer culture that has long overwhelmed any subtle and real flavors with loads of tomato ketchup and refined sugars to such a point where vegetables taste "boring" and water "disgusting." Our "much-loved" kids keep spending all their days in a sterile, square room without smells or tastes and with nothing to touch. Nothing to do for the body all day, while the brain fills up with unwanted, unexperienced second-hand data. A boy who fidgets, dying to get active with his body, is diagnosed as ADHD and filled with Ritulin to keep him "normal."

The way out of the progressive loss of our senses would of course be to start using them and to allow them their natural place. Particularly our children need to be allowed to taste, smell, touch, and feel the natural world around them—not just seeing and hearing about it—if they are to become real humans instead of mental freaks that cannot feel, taste, smell, or touch! This should be obvious to anybody with some intelligence, as using all of our senses equally has to be at the very core of what ought to be "common sense."

An intelligent type of school would go even further and possibly *connect* the various sensory systems. Why not assign a letter, flavor, fragrance, touch, and musical note to every number, and thus integrate all learning? The letter A could equal 1=C Maj=taste of salt =smell of apples =touch of a wooden ball=feeling of undividedness. But first, we need to teach chemistry via smelling cut grass and cow-dung, cooking by smelling what we cook, medicine by knowing the unhealthy smells and so forth! The first, and most essential step of schools in the future, would have to be the introduction of *six-dimensional learning*, which will of course bring with it a tendency towards outdoor classes and fundamental priority changes in the curriculum. The sense of smell, which is known to connect to infinitely detailed memory, can be used to open up windows and doors to unbelievable dimensions of perception and memory that we have utterly ignored because we learn as little from our dogs as we do from our children. To use the five generally conscious senses for learning instead of only the two increases a child's learning potential by a factor of 2.5 and it changes an arbitrary, selective view of the universe into a wholesome and fundamentally more human view. If we include intuition, the inner sense, which could include meditation classes and self-observation, we will not only *triple* our children's learning, but also end the current and historic suppression of their joy and the perpetuation of culturally imposed imbalances! This learning via all the senses comes quite naturally with travel, where children meet with hundreds of new flavors and smells every day, and where they can touch their world in so many new ways. Who wants to wait for schools to discover the meaning of common sense, while our kids could go touch a baby elephant, smell fallen mangoes on the forest floor, taste a self-caught fish, and know in their guts what they feel inside?

But what can a responsible parent do who is tied to a job where he can't travel? He can break all the rules that limit freedom unnecessarily and simply focus the kids' attention on smells in the kitchen, the bathroom, the garden, or play smell and taste recognition games with eyes tied in the forest.

Or he can play outdoor chess with his children when they are little! Chess-kids develop their minds better when they touch and move big wooden pieces around! It improves their confidence! Their self-respect! The world of smells is then all around them while they use their brains. Or we could make chess pieces of different fragrant woods, without varnish, and well-textured! Round scales for bishops, square scales for rooks...This would not only connect children to the kinetic sense but also allow the blind to learn chess faster and enjoy it more.

Eventually, when children have learned to accept the rules and developed enough discipline—they will be getting ready to break a few of those limiting rules themselves, discard some of our own narrow world-views and drop their automatic awe for what parents and teachers believe. They can now sometimes beat their teacher or father and manifest their superior awareness! Now they may not always listen to adults' various ideas on chess or life—after beating those ideas regularly.

At this stage, a child can no longer be programmed by just any adult into believing a thing he hasn't verified for himself. He seeks his own truths now, beyond what everybody else says...and that is then his own self-chosen and self-responsible path to self-awareness and mind-development!

To stifle this natural path is what really creates the "crazy teenager" and the so-called "difficult kids," by transferred definition!

Kids need not only learn some rules, but also that it is okay to break those rules on occasion. As a rule, the queen has higher value and more power than a knight—but this is not always so! Sometimes this rule does not apply but needs to be broken and the queen sacrificed!

Just like, as a rule, a kid should obey his father, when he organizes family matters. But not always! Sometimes the father is wrong and then the son needs to put his foot down or speak up and do things his own way, if he is to grow up. He needs to learn the value of rules—and the value of their breaking as well! He may really dislike doing the dishes. So, he offers to do the cooking instead, inspired by master chef Ainsley. He is possibly never asked to do dishes again.

As a rule, my girls knew, I usually saw more options on the board and understand chess better than they did. But they also knew that by looking really well, they would sometimes see things more clearly than I and then come out tops! They knew the rule of my superior competence could be broken, and they loved breaking this rule on the board, or when fishing or in an argument. And this never lost me any of their respect...

Their ability to break the rules, without arrogantly discarding those rules for no good reason, is what I was always proud of, as it showed me their grit, their true self-reliance.

Are you worried that this might undermine your authority and lead to chaos? Then try breaking a few rules yourself! Like the ones imposed by your own imposing father and teacher that still rule your life, or those rules of politically correct, two-dimensional society that still keep you from using all your senses and from thinking for yourself...

Ask your teenager when she comes home late why she did that and accept a good reason respectfully! It then becomes much easier for her to escape the rules of her role of submissive daughter and easier to emotionally understand why you would worry sometimes.

You can either help your kids in growing up while they break your rules, or you can fight them every step of the way...

On the chess-board you can actually do both! It is okay to present all your experience and knowledge here and to fully show your insights! But when your seven-year old begins to outwit you on occasion, breaking all the rules of experienced adult strategy, to win games against you and against the odds—then comes a time where you must realize that you don't always know best! Be proud of that and accept what your kid is showing you here!

A good draw is often better than attempting to win at all cost.

It may just help you doing what your kids are supposed to help you with—to break those rules that don't work for you and to grow up yourself!

Chapter 13: Sex and Chess

There was this guy in our chess club who would never have sex before a competition.

"If I have sex before chess, I'm all wiped out, but if I keep it in, I'm ready to fight like a rooster," was his often-crowed conviction.

Many of us cocked up at that, and he being a rather successful player, our girl-friends suffered...

This man is definitely not alone. Many sportsmen hold this belief and let the juices accumulate before the event. Are they right or is this one hell of a male delusion, that only distracts from performance? And how on earth does this relate to parenting?

Sex-education is the weakest aspect of parenting in the western world! It is what almost all parents have the most difficulties with. This is because sex, like all really important life-skills, is not taught, not considered important enough, and because nobody knows much of any relevance about it! This has to change, if children are to take us seriously and become competent for life! What we all need is actual competence before we start to speak! Or else we will at this stage be seen by our children as the hypocrites we really are! Apart from this, sex is of course the path to create life and to make love, and thus of ultimate importance in forming any world view! It should therefore be treated as an art, a science, a religious ritual, and as the most natural thing in the world.

Apart from tai chi and acupuncture, the old Taoist masters left us with another great and little-received gift—the art of love-making! This art has for thousands of years been kept very secret because of its dangers to the uninitiated but is today being rediscovered. The secret is to use sexual energy (Jing Chi) and to suck it up the spine on inhalation, instead of ejaculating it.

The Chinese see sexuality not as a threat or as a consumer-product, but as an interplay of fire and water where the female vessel contains the water, heated by the male fire underneath. Fire burns quickly, but water heats up slowly. Or it should.... But when the man reaches the point of orgasm, all his energy leaks out and is then no longer available. He is exhausted. Game over. He is defeated. Woman barely lukewarm...

A tantra practitioner, standing in a chi kung stance, inhales, sucking his orgasmic energy back into the tail bone which has two little holes for that purpose, then up the spine until he feels a tingle in the top of his skull...

If now the anal muscles are squeezed, this tingle can become very strong and flush the brain like a bright water fountain. This can lead to new insights and life-altering light experiences...It most certainly is a formidable tool for self-development that must not be ignored!

There are however strict, highly disciplined rules to this practise, as the energies handled can be many tens of thousands of Volt. It must be practised with cold energy first, before using hot (aroused) energy. So, careful here!

The effect of retaining semen is that orgasm does not end in a steep downward curve of energy, but becomes a plateau, where we can remain for hours. It can be experienced in any body-part we choose, like the kidneys, the heart or the brain, simply by directing it there via breath and visualization.

Sexual energy is in fact identical with life energy and mental energy, and sex is quite proportional to intelligence, as Henry Miller has much enjoyed pointing out!

With a little practise, this Taoist tantra can become the *most* powerful of all our tools for self-development and enables us to work with energy directly, either to heal or to love, to see, to work, to study—for any purpose. Should the breathing and visualization aspects of this practise not be taught at schools?

Should a parent not study up on what actually *matters*, well beyond our consumerist pleasures, before embarking on our so-called "sex-education?" If we are serious about reaching our child's potential, we cannot possibly do without harnessing the strongest biological and motivational force at human disposal! How unusual that must sound inside a culture that has evolved from the suppression and the bedevilment of sex...but it is the truth—the most ignored truth.

Regular practise of this so-called "semen kung-fu" means that sexual energy, normally wasted in conventional ten-second orgasms, becomes now available for other purposes, including the development of brain-power! This practise has nothing at all to do with sex, does not lead to "sexualization" of a child; it is only about breathing, visualization and becoming conscious of energy movements in the body! Apart from loading us up with energy, this preparation for semen- or ovarian kung-fu often leads to quantum jumps in understanding and even intelligence! It makes a huge difference to our performance in all fields and to the development of teenagers who, wise to their own sexuality, discover independence, self-acceptance, out-of-the-box thinking, real knowledge and accelerated self-development, while running no risk with abusive sex or unwanted pregnancies. Actual sex is then not the only option for teens to explore their sexual energy!

In chess, whether ejaculation before a competition game is "good" or "bad" will depend on a player's nervous disposition. For nervous, excited or tense players, sex can have a calming and relaxing effect which might improve their game. But for men who run out of stamina and mental freshness, feeling tired too quickly, ejaculatory sex before a game will not work. They are better off having non-ejaculatory sex or do tantric chi kung.

During a game, or in class, thoughts of sex are obviously distracting, but there is a technique called "riding the tiger," that can quickly restore mental energy to a tiring player: Just squeeze the anal muscles twenty-five times, relaxing between squeezes, while sitting upright. The spine needs to be aligned in a straight position for chi to rise through it uninhibited, the chin tucked in and the tongue touching the roof of the mouth.

It is also quite puzzling to your opponent when you re-energize like that, especially if you adopt a chi kung stance while at it. He will rightly suspect some mysterious magic, much like the presence of Russian parapsychologists at world championships...

So yes, it is true what this guy said about fighting like a rooster! Work with your sexual energy, be sexy, but keep it in and transform it into mental freshness! Don't waste it! It will triple your energy-levels!

Nor crow too much about it unless you wish to face all your chess-opponents squeezing their anuses while you play them...

Since these exercises don't require intercourse or a partner, they are in principle the best and the only tool for the sex-driven teenager to convert surplus sexual energy (jing chi) into school-work, character-development and superior health, as well as chess prowess and success at sports. It protects a hundred per cent from STDs and pregnancy, provides the ultimate safety and control we all seek, and yet lets teenagers explore their sexuality as a *positive*, constructive, self-owned and creative force that need never be suppressed!! This is why it needs to be taught!

If you feel strange or ignorant about teaching teenagers positively about sex, you may prefer to leave it to the school, to institutionalized religious contempt for sex, or to the speculations of the peer-group. Who will answer the undeniably existing questions? You may even believe sex should not be taught at all, since they're going to find out anyway...

But they don't! Apart from the tantric secret knowledge from China and Tibet, there is no constructive source of information out there! By consulting our western pornography, other teenagers, and those adults who simply don't know anything beyond the mechanical, they cannot possibly find any answers except the frightening advice on STDs, pregnancy, and on what to expect in ten minutes of copulation. This Abrahamic contempt for sex in our Christian, Jewish and Muslim societies, and the utter lack of relevant knowledge, is what leads to all of those problems with uninformed, blindly exploring teenagers!

If you are at all serious about getting your moves right as a parent and about avoiding

major errors—you need to passively teach sexuality from early childhood, guided by the

questions as they arise, not any agenda, and as naturally competent as you are in other areas.

It starts with "potty-training" really. There are parents who think that verbal instructions

will eventually teach their baby, or that it is simply a matter of waiting out the "phase."

Get real! Babies and small kids learn from example, not from talking! They need to be

shown! If they don't have an older sibling who masters the art of using potty, you need to show them yourself! Yes, oh you much dignified parent—get a second potty, sit

together, listen together, actually produce a visible result and be proud together! That

is how a baby will learn quickest!

The sane parent needs to also ask—how is a boy supposed to learn how to piss these days, with daddy always doing it in a locked-up, "private" cubicle?? These things need to be shown to a little boy in a positive manner, with the support of a tree, rather than leaving him for months in nappies, waiting for his eventual enlightenment or for a dog to show up and broaden his horizons!

As always, you yourself need to learn first what you wish your kid to be competent about! Don't talk about things you don't really understand! Find out the potential and the sacred beauty of this

God-given gift that is your own sexuality, develop yourself and then treat sex like all other areas of conversation! To start with—get over your cultural conditioning to see sex as a dirty or sinful thing that needs to be kept away from children!

You may feel a bit "technical" or distracted from your expression of love when you first concentrate on the flow of energy. It is the same in chess, when you first face a lot of rules and techniques to learn, long before you achieve the mastery of playing without a thought, the Zen way, the Tao way. It is the same with every craft or art under the sun! Why should sex be an exception? Why is sex not being taught??

The chess-player can appreciate a set of rules as to conduct, and willingly learn some artful techniques with great interest. How hard can it then be for him to realize that in sex as well, you need to go through an apprenticeship before you can become a master?

But should you really teach your teenager the secrets of Chinese sexuality, when they've already become incapable to swerve their heads away from pornography and when they don't want to talk about it with their parents?

As always, you need to teach yourself in the *first* place, for your own benefit and energy, which will transform you from a tired, worn-out parent into a fit, energetic player that kids can look up to, and who has a happy partner full of deep respect and content! This will give you the competence necessary for your teenager to look up and eventually ask you anything about health and sex. It makes what you then speak truthful and sufficiently interesting.

To deny sexuality in the young or to teach them mostly to "say no" is a nonsense that never ever works, never has, and never will! They just think you "over the hill." What we need to teach them instead is what we ourselves had never suspected—that sexual energy and mental energy are one and the same! I myself was able to quickly increase my IQ from 140 to 165 through these exercises and my chess from Elo

2000 to 2100. Like all really good and really fundamental things, sex has to be a part of competent living and of competent parenting!

But the main blessing is to stay natural and unembarrassed about sexuality, which keeps the teenager talking and sane, and on your side!

Then and only then can a parent help his teenagers deal with their sexuality issues competently and prevent the solitary, often suicidal kid that cannot cope with the challenges of facing alone what the rest of society ignores and therefore fears and condemns.

Yes, you should teach sexuality as a positive and divine art, instead of just a dangerous and problematic hormonal thing that should be suppressed and could kill you. You avoid all those problems like STDs and unwanted pregnancies this way, and—you give your teenager the finest tool for self-development that ever existed!

Never force this kind of knowledge on teenagers though! Wait until they ask why you are so happy and relaxed, and so fit compared to other parents. And then still keep most of your Chinese secret knowledge to yourself and let them surf the internet for more, just to make it harder and thus more personally valuable, and to allow them to discover it for themselves *first*...Tell them only what they have worked hard to find out and what they are ready for, just as in chess!

You will find they will like good, clean and powerful knowledge about sex much more than the pornography, the commercial nonsense, and the all-negative "sex education" they find elsewhere!

To such a teenager, the issue of gender choice is no issue either! In chess, every pawn is a transsexual. When it "matures" at the end of its path to the other side of the board it has a choice into what it will transform. Most popular is to transform into a queen, but it could be a horse if appropriate. The gender of a pawn is similarly open to transformation as is human gender. Today's overidentification with gender is just another expression of our either-or mentality, whereas in reality all humans are as embryos female and as adults *both* male and female! Females have male sex-hormones and vice versa. Humans get reborn as male and female throughout time. To think of oneself as purely female or purely male is incorrect and causes huge, and entirely preventable identity conflicts.

Now that I've done the crowing—I leave you to grow your own mind about what sexuality really is and can be, and how to easily and naturally discuss it with your now actually interested teenager.

If you yourself have the necessary competence as a parent, you can prevent sexual disorientation completely, or at least face your horny teenager and topics like sex-change, homosexuality and pornography with positive wisdom and oriented dignity.

Chapter 14: Body and fitness

A healthy mind usually lives in a healthy body, with apologies to possible exceptions, like Steven Hawking. The brain is part of that body, not anything apart from it. And the body is part of mind, where every cell has its own intelligence, its own memory.

If we want to play chess well, this mind/body has to be fit, well oxygenated and relaxed. The nervous system particularly needs to be well balanced and strong, the eyes clear and fresh.

Fashionably, when we think about health, we focus mostly on the dietary approach, which is only one factor out of many.

First of all, your weight as such does not make the slightest difference to good health or to your chess game! Although everybody talks about weight in a health context all the time, it has absolutely nothing to do with health. Think of the African matron pounding maize with an infant slung over her shoulders, weighing in at a hundred-and-twenty kilo, whose body is much harder, fitter and better than the average eighteen-year old from England at fifty kg!

What could be wrong with a hundred-and-twenty kg of hard muscular flesh? Is Serena Williams overweight at whatever she may weigh? I suggest Barbie-doll is the one underweight, and our own brains without a doubt!

The problem is of course never weight, but fat, one of those much-avoided truths!

"Fat" is such a barbed word today that young western females have just about banned it from the dictionary! Eighteen-year old girls from England are nearly always fat, even when they are not overweight at all. To be fat is a health problem even if the person is skinny, as it reduces oxygen and fitness considerably. The solution is to throw away the scales and pinch your arm instead. If it is flabby, you are fat and lazy; if it is muscular you are good! Weight has zilch to do with it!

This is the first point to make on young people's good health, from the sober perspective of a chess-player.

Another point may then be the nutrients. Certainly, you need fat, protein and carbs, we all know that. What matters much more, is the natural quality of those nutrients and the addition of genuine vitamins, chlorophyll, enzymes, minerals and micro-organisms.

If your eggs come from battery hens fed on antibiotics, and your meat from a pig that never sees the sun-light or a blade of grass, or feel any feelings of freedom in its entire life, you may get all the nutrients science is talking about, but you will be no healthier than that poor, caged pig and the caged, abused and joyless chickens...

And thirdly, if you eat only the muscle (steaks, roasts) of an animal, you will get ill over time, just like a chess-position where only two pieces are used, but if you eat all the parts, like the brain, the marrow, the inner organs—none of the meat-eater ailments will likely befall you as you are in a natural balance.

This is what matters, not your calorie intake, which is quite meaningless.

Generally, our food science and our nutritional beliefs are just the latest form materialism has taken. We are not so much what we eat, but rather what we *think* and *feel*! Our thoughts and attitudes influence health far more than what we eat, especially with children!

Just to go for a moment with what most people are already aware of, here are a few dietary pointers that may make some difference to performance and growth in chess-players and teenagers:

Eat lots of parsley and green leafy vegetables, which are the primary brain food! Add root vegetables like carrots, which according to Rudolf Steiner feed the brain, as the inverted form of plants corresponds to the human form.

You can add walnuts, whose shape closely imitates the brain, and you can eat gingko seeds (quite bitter, though!).

The best food to keep illnesses like untimely flues and colds away is—ginger! Nothing better for general health! Garlic is good for that too, but not before a game. This is cheating. And your teen is just going to roll her eyes in disbelief at such a suggestion...

Right before a game, it is best not to eat too much in the way of fat and protein, but to stick to fruit sugars as in dried fruit or an apple (very crunchy ones are great strategy, just short of cheating!). It may pay to have a gram of vitamin C before a competition but be aware that vitamin C tablets are not the same as the vitamins from a well-grown fresh fruit, which is much preferable.

Don't give too much of your attention to diet though, just be aware of what your body needs. Take responsibility, find out the truth about food and *observe*—it is always the same drill.

What *you* know and understand, your children will soon know as well.

Never force your kids to eat anything! Simply don't buy rubbish.

What kids need from your example is to see how to evaluate the life-force in food and to develop a subtle sense of taste that would be lost by drinking refined sugars and soft-drinks. An active kid does however need plenty of natural sugars and high-quality protein and oils as in fish and nuts.

Apart from correct diet there are a few helpful things you can do to improve performance on the chess-board or before exams: a very good one is the shoulder- or the headstand, where the blood can flood and freshen up the brain. This should be done regularly but is very good just before the game.

Yoga can be the answer for nervous players. Chi kung and yoga strengthen the nervous system, relax deeply, oxygenate the body and foster a collected, calm disposition. These exercises are a lot more effective than any mind-designed diet when it comes to chess or to other sport.

For smaller kids, martial arts and dancing are usually more suited than Yoga, as they need physical activity to learn.

During a game, or in front of a computer, there is a big difference between sitting upright and slouching forward! When the spine is not straight, chi cannot travel well from the bottom to the top of the spinal column and you will tire quickly. So, sit upright, but not tensely. Keep up your own example when your kid slouches!

For a really fast increase of mental energy we have our anal squeezes. This can be further supplemented by other quick-fix manoeuvres. You can press the fleshy part between thumb and index finger to increase well-being and you can touch your temples for better concentration. But what works better is rubbing your ears until they redden! This is almost as strong as sending sexual energy to the brain, and your opponent or your kid's school-mate isn't left guessing where the sudden blush comes from...

Teach these ancient "tricks" to your kid, to use before exams and before sport games and performances! Yes, even the anal squeezes—they beat chemicals by a mile!

Smoking may reduce oxygen intake and be the crutch of a teenager lacking self-acceptance, but it does not noticeably interfere with chess. Neither does, strangely enough, alcohol when consumed in some moderation or by Bavarians.

Asians should avoid alcohol almost entirely and I'm no more being racist here than I was sexist a mile back. It is simply what is on the board.

To young Asian and Polynesian people, alcohol is poison!

To teenagers, alcohol is more a mental and attitudinal danger than a physical one. Drinking alcohol regularly and also smoking foster self-indulgence and can completely destroy the warrior attitude in a young person!

To try a little sip of beer and wine however is okay, especially for very little kids! It is only what you keep secret and reserved for adulthood, that kids learn most to want! Treat beer, like all other food, with respect and moderation, and it will never come to symbolize freedom, free time, initiation or adult gratification.

Sport is a very good and necessary addition to chess. Our physical fitness is what determines our mental fitness. The right sports will be aerobic, not muscle-bound. It is all about increasing the oxygen in our bodies and the stamina to keep going for five to seven hours without tiring.

I found Boris Spassky a particularly bright example of physical/ mental fitness. I met the ex- world champion at a simultaneous play in Augsburg, Germany. The man exuded a full-on physical presence, smiled a lot, inter-acted charmingly with his beautiful, sexy French wife, while answering questions, and he always played some hard games of tennis before competition. A good man to learn from, I thought! Spassky has that palpable, room-filling quality of being here, now in his body, and he was pumped with energy. Even his head was of normal size and shape, quite an accomplishment for a grandmaster...

Of much greater importance than diet or sport is correct breathing! Most people think breathing or sex come naturally and need not be learned. This is a monumental error!

These two basic human activities deserve and need training more than all others, since almost nobody has a clue about the potential of sex or of breathing! To breathe correctly, one has to sit up straight, so that both belly and chest are unrestricted and can fully fill up. Some people, especially office-workers and school-kids find this quite difficult and distracting and soon they breathe like sick old versions of themselves. Sitting straight is a most fundamental life-skill that needs to be most carefully monitored in children and young people.

It can help in severe cases to seek a practitioner of re-birthing, who can restore the naturally perfect rhythm of their breathing, deepening it to exactly the right level. But relaxed long runs in the woods also balance the rhythm, and without external help.

To just meditate on normal breathing is a further way to achieve such results.

What seems to matter most about the body and the mind is their degree of connectedness! If the mind looks down at the body as something other than self, there can only be separateness and division. We need to realize that mind, body and soul are not distinct and separate things, but three manifestations of the one being we are; three ways of looking at reality, not three realities! Once we understand this, we can more easily achieve that Oneness between body and mind. A cat can do it because it doesn't split up reality by thinking. Its mind knows it is body...

And Boris Spassky can obviously do it, despite the fact that his and our culture is built on an either/or duality that has split our personalities into groups of irreconcilable opposites like mind or body, left or right, old or young. It's all in the divided attitude.

Many minds however now look at their bodies with disgust or vanity, as arbitrarily distributed objects, as if the body were object and possession rather than the expression and residence of mind and created by mind.

Some even feel "trapped" inside a body of the "wrong" gender instead of facing the challenges proposed by the gender their soul has chosen for a good reason!

But as phrenology, iridology, blood-tests and all physiological processes clearly show—the body expresses and represents the mind of a person to the point of identity with that mind. Every wrinkle, every symptom and every smile correspond to feelings or attitudes of the mind! The body is thus not something we "have," but instead something we are." Realizing this, ends our inner-most division, which makes us instantly a whole lot better at the art of playing chess and at the great game of parenting...

The teenager, whose parent understands these fundamental realities, enjoys a real preparation for life, does not fall for illusions easily and has a solid basis from which to master her life. She understands that to look after the body is to cultivate mind and self-responsibility.

By seeing these connections, the parent can get even a five-year old to do really well at kung fu, chi kung, chess, or mental exercise games—whatever the family plays with passion and enthusiasm!

After all—a little boy can develop "superpowers" by training like Jacky Chan and other masters, can he not?

Yes. That is right. He can...

Chapter 15: Teenagers and playing for draw

Parenting children feels to a loving and intelligent parent much like gardening does to the gardener. It is not work.

Kids need to be embedded in the right soil, given the right amount of water, sunshine and shelter, nutrients and grooming. And you are the gardener, the one in control, and the one at fault if the plant does not grow into a strong, healthy young tree. You are proud of every twig your child grows and feel responsible for that.

You are God-like! The Creator of your child!

And then she reaches puberty and becomes a teenager!!

Your world crumbles, the God cracks and becomes the old dog...You're losing the game! What has happened, you then ask, while you watch your young trees grow legs and jump in and out of your garden and of your total control.

Now is the time to quickly drop the idea of "nurturing a plant!" You may have been a wonderful gardener until now—but it is wild game you're feeding now, not lettuces!

You need an entirely new view of your teenage child at this stage, a new definition for your relationship. You need to figure out what a teenager really is and how to parent this new creature effectively. You need a new perspective of the game you're playing, or you will quickly lose...

Parenting teenagers is a bit like shooting an arrow in a storm! First, you enjoyed this feeling of great control, while you were pulling that bow and started to take aim. But from the moment the arrow flies, into its own life, you have lost all control!

You will not fully accept that and twist with your body to influence the flight of the long-lost arrow, right until it either meets your will, hitting your mark—or you give up on it and try to find it in the grass later...

Teenagers are arrows with little awareness of who fired them or where they are going.

They reckon they've been flying forever!

And this view point is of course just as valid as ours—that of the archer! Or a baby's perspective for that matter. They all live in different space/time continuums, that distort emotional space differently.

As it is with a mayfly or a mosquito, our teenagers' time experience is simply different from ours, even though we share the same space. The party tomorrow is the *only* party to go to *ever! Everybody* is going to be there!

The teenager lives here/now as does the arrow! This is what they are trying to tell us and this is what we don't understand, simply because we discern no awareness in them of where they are going, of what they are going to hit next, and of where they (bloody!) came from! And because we ourselves have forgotten how to fly...

There are of course still those things we parents are needed for. We need to point at consequences, at how you can get hurt, and tell the old stories of how we got hurt.

We nurture their souls as best we understand. But we also need to respect and learn from the strengths of our teenager, instead of just anointing her as "crazy" and writing her off for the duration of what we ignorantly see as a "phase" we can wait out!

The only way a teenager is going to continue listening to you, is for you to listen first, and listen well and gain insights from her perspective, instead of commenting from your unchangeable position that will never budge, no matter what she can say...

This is the precise point where parents fall short of setting the required example for true respect—and then complain of a disrespectful teenager who now equally talks down to them in just the same patronizing way.

What you need to do now is respect your teenager's tantrums as emotional birth-pains, where she practices aspects of self! The less you oppose these struggles of the larva, the sooner the butterfly is going to fly!

This is the time to play for draw instead of trying to win a losing game! Build a sleep-out at the far end of your section, a kind of lawless zone, where she is sole queen in her guaranteed privacy and where she can project and act out various "adult" emotions and dramas! When she understands you're still on her side and respectful of how she feels, no matter how irrational that may appear—only then will she hear, heed and respect what you say and empathize with your own needs and feelings as a parent.

That is the whole "trick," the never fathomed secret that still allows you to keep the game going.

Teenagers only appear insane to parents who take their own position and that of their culture as all there is and can be. They don't know better than we do, they just notice better than we do what is wrong with us and with our society. They are like film critics who cannot (yet) make a better film but can detect all the little faults and errors in the film we have made. We can either be offended and annoyed by that, or we can make good use of their criticism.

By taking a teenager's critique seriously and by occasionally responding with change, we are showing the necessary respect for the child to feel heard and to feel some power to influence the world, without needing to fully commit to rebellion.

Thus, making *sense* of the "phase" and discovering meaning in what most parents today experience as teenage insanity, allows us to avoid alienation and to maintain the flow of communication.

To get stuck with the routine parental role-play of always knowing best, based on experience, and to always admonish and direct and advise, is a strategy leading unerringly to check-mate in a few moves. It keeps the teenager stuck in his (so far unsuccessful!) rebellion and the parent stuck in a world-view where children have nothing to teach, while we have every right to impose our views on them. This creation of the classic Oedipus-syndrome forces a son to then emotionally "kill his father," just to assert his own reality and feel his own way...

It is much better strategy to go with change and simply accept, and then understand the view-point of your critic and his generation as valid.

Teenagers are not at all in a "crazy phase," nor do their opinions come from a lack of brain-development. Humans of all ages have equal potential for awareness.

They do things not because they amount to financial, material or even "common" sense as we call it, but because they need to figure out their own definitions, their own emotional connection to actions. Their logic is based on the exploration of possibilities, not on what works from experience.

They take drugs because they want to experience all there is to experience in the world, and that is why they roller-skate and listen to music too.

They get pregnant because that is life uncensored and because that is what their bodies, their hearts and nature tell them to do. They haven't internalized yet that western society expects, for cultural reasons, a sixteen-year old girl to be the sole care provider for her child, which is far too young for such a sole charge...

She rebels against that because her instincts and her body tell her of biological realities where child-birth is easier at sixteen than it is at twenty-six and where it should be "normal," as it is natural, for a baby to be raised by the extended family and the village community, rather than by any single woman! She feels the system is wrong and listens to how things feel to her—and gets pregnant!

The resulting "disaster" is one of cultural definition, projected to be the teenage girl's fault, who is then made to feel like a slut rather than allowed to be a proud mother.

Teenagers get into our faces, because we are so vain that we refuse to realize that we too need to "grow up" in this relationship! Grow up, not physically or to function in a given society, but to develop into fully mature human beings.

We never practice what we preach, and our teenagers are masters in pointing that out. Check!

Or they stop talking if we won't hear of it…Game over.

The "successful" teenager manages to get the parent into a crisis, making him face his own words applied to himself, all his weaknesses and his hypocrisies the bull's eye for his little girl's darts… You can now either sulk and age fast, or you can ask yourself "am I fully seeing the world as it really is?"

As parents, we usually deny this crisis, deny the call to grow up, deny fearing to lose our child to ways frightening to us. And this denial leads us to blame the "crazy teenager" for our own inner pains and errors!

We must beware of a godlike view, where children are "unfinished" or "unready" little adults, with less awareness than we do in all things. Teenagers are not, as psychologist/comedian Nigel Latta proclaimed on NZTV "simply insane, and the brain not working properly. They may look like us, but they are not really people!" He continued to describe teens as complete idiots, to the immense delight and utter relief of the parent-audience. Sad man, really.

This view of children and teenagers is very consistent with our attitudes towards animals and it is one of those points on our to-do list for growing up!

Parents and teenagers raise each other, to be realistic! They present equal challenge to each other in regard of their world views and their human awareness.

Children are just as perfect for their age as we suppose we are, even more so.

They haven't fucked up yet! We have.

They haven't given up on part of their genetic potential yet. We have.

They are not unfinished adults. We ourselves are old children, who never grew beyond our fears and illusions towards what our genes might well have allowed!

Can you be grateful to your teenager who, in code, hints at the squareness of your horizons and deflates what you thought was *it*? Can you still alter your view-point? Those are the questions that need asking if we are to close the "generation-gap" that we ourselves have created!

You can never win the game of raising your teenager by following your design and game-plan! All you can do is play for draw.

Look at each position from both sides—through the eyes of black and white, parent and kid—until you can equally see both sides of that *one* truth! Look until you see *all there is*, rather than select what you have always identified with!

And this is the aim of raising a teenager—you both escape the narrowness of your ages and perspectives and learn to see *both* sides of the story—which is to be an adult.

Then there is no generation conflict. No opponents with opposing mind-sets, no rebellion, no "crazy" teenager! No black and white! Nobody trying to win at all cost. You are no longer crazy and you won't drive your teen crazy...

Your teenager now knows you as the one who released the arrow, the one aiming and holding the bow, back there.

Now he can fly truly free.

Is that not what you wanted, back there?

Can you now remember how to fly?

That is how much he helped you grow up, your teenager!

Chapter 16: Patience and Non-waiting

In a world made of appearances, many people wonder at the patience of chess-players "waiting" for their opponent's move and ponder the boredom they themselves would feel in their place.

Those same people also view fishing as boring, where they suppose you wait for hours just to get a nibble, while doing nothing...

They "wait" for hours at airports, they "wait" during nine months of pregnancy, they "wait" to see what happens, can't wait to have children, and then "wait" for them to "grow up."

And, of course, they will then always tell their children to "wait" until they are older...

Parents who "wait," call all the most important, personality-evolving times in their children's lives "phases," meaning they're just going to go away by themselves! They are not to be taken seriously and just have to be waited out!

By doing so, they completely miss the meaning and purpose of what is going on during the "stubborn phase" of their two-year old, and they will later completely avoid facing the challenges teenagers pose to their parental ego. They just wait for the "phase" to be over, suspending their parental responsibilities.

There is no waiting in life! Waiting is to be dead until a certain event resurrects you!

Waiting is complete tunnel-vision.

The chess-player never waits! The time his opponent takes is his own time also, to make full use of! He visualizes options, no matter whose turn it is, and when his partner finally moves, he has already considered that option and now needs little more time. He is always fully on the ball and never has cause to wait for anything.

Fishing similarly may look quiet to an onlooker, but the fisherman doesn't "wait". When he is not busy cutting up bait, observing the weather, the anchor-line, the feeding patterns, the sea-birds, the changing breeze, and when the bait and burley are well-placed—then he feels the depth of the water and the secrets and magical possibilities of the ocean just by touching that fishing-line that connects him to the deep water and to unforeseeable sudden contacts with *life!* He is as ready to respond as is the panther or any hunter and he is certainly not "bored," while standing or sitting poised and still for some time.

The chess-player and the fisherman are full-on hunters. They don't wait. They are just patient and therefore effective. Patience is not doing and not waiting!

When you wait, you do nothing and you are bored. But patience means to stay prepared, to see the work and to enjoy getting it done, without expecting instant results or reward.

In parenting, there is never a good time for waiting either! Waiting for what? A better future? For kids to grow out of their childhood?

Don't wait with understanding your baby until it speaks!

Don't tell your three-year old son to "wait until he is older," when he touches a knife. Teach about knives as you would to a three-year-old man instead!

When he asks you about sex at age four—never postpone the answers until later, when he is going to get them from a six-year old. Give honest answers now, while *keeping the questions alive!*

When your daughter wants to join karate at age four, don't tell her to wait! You already waited too long...

When you spend five hours at an airport—invent people-observation games, like who looks happy and who uncomfortable and why, or whether noses indicate character-traits, and you will see time fly for you and your well-entertained kids. But if you'd tell them to sit down on those chairs for five hours and "wait" without making ill-mannered noises, then they'd soon show you just how crazy they can drive you!

Patience is not watching the hard-to-accept with grinding teeth or bearing the "burdens of parenthood".

Patience is to accept those quantum-jump developmental times in children as real and necessary and to work with the challenges to our ego and world-view without flying into rages or turning away.

Patience is non-waiting. It is to bide the time until the perfect moment and it is the basis of effective tactical action.

If your teenager already is in a frenzy of emotional accusations and you already feel like shit—then you have waited too long and you likely still lack the patience to hear what she has to say. Yelling back then proves beyond doubt your inability and lack of understanding. There is never a good reason for "spanking" or yelling at children or teenagers! It does not work and it is entirely destructive. It teaches yelling as a way out from reasonable dialogue and it teaches violence, non-listening and disrespect.

To practice non-waiting is not the same as "doing," however! Non-waiting is to recognize the opportunities, to observe what is going on. It does not mean you interfere.

When kids fight with each other, for example—to just stop them would be impatient and a "doing" from which they can't learn a thing. They don't learn to solve conflict by being stopped, nor will they find to self-responsibility.

But to observe the nature of the conflict and to propose intelligent solutions—that is non-waiting!

Where you have already waited long enough to have a demanding, spoiled and obnoxious brat of a kid, you cannot suddenly "correct" this by losing your patience!

It was your own fault after all.

Just make the right moves from now on and save the game before it is lost!

Or reset and try afresh, without the handicap of waiting for better days.

Kids are quite patient really, unless you keep them waiting...

Chapter 17: Chess as meditation

Chess is commonly associated with concentration, which is the opposite of meditation. It plainly is not, by its nature, a meditation. In concentration, we focus our attention onto one subject, one focal point. In meditation, we detach ourselves from any one particular point of interest and expand our attention to the Whole or to the Nothing.

So how can chess have anything to do with meditation?

Nobody has ever snapped into a state of meditation by *trying* to meditate, especially not a teenager! To try meditating implies and creates obstacles. Trying generally creates resistance and seriousness and distance and thus slows us down. We can therefore not sit down and do anything directly to get into a state of meditation, least of all plan or think our way towards it.

The trick is to start with the opposite! If you want strong yang—start with gentle yin! If you want to jump high, bend your knees first and lower yourself! If you want your kid to explore something—forbid or hide it! This is how to practically apply the law of yin and yang, the two forces that grow and diminish constantly to become each other.

What does this mean in terms of how to meditate?

It means that it is best to start with the opposite! You concentrate on a point, like a mandala or a chess board. After a while, the brain gets tired, especially those cognitive parts in the front left cortex that we don't need in meditation. Then doors begin to open up, and windows that allow us to go into this other world called meditation.

Every good musician transcends the concentration of thinking what her fingers will do next and then just flows with the music, empty of thought or ownership. That is how to do it! This is how to master all things.

There is a wonderful meditation, where the yoga teacher tells his seated students to do nothing and just let the body breathe itself. It never works!

I found a way, while teaching yoga to the locals in the rural Philippines, that *always* worked:

You let the person run hard out along the beach, until you're sure they're out of breath. Then sit them down against a tree, while still puffing like bag-pipes, and tell them to let their body alone do all the breathing and – *witness it*! Now everybody can of course do it, even on the very first attempt! After a while, when their hearts have already slowed down, they are still sitting there—observing their bodies breathe themselves!

Starting thus with the opposite works every time and gets people into *actual* meditation.

And this is the secret of why chess is such a formidable entrance into a state of total awareness, where concentration becomes meditation—in order to achieve something, we must start from its opposite! High activity is a good basis for stillness—and meditation is the mother of supreme concentration...

If you tell a kid to sit still, he itches to move! If you do this to an energetic boy regularly, he will show the symptoms of what we then call ADHD. There is nothing at all wrong with that boy and everything wrong with the expectation of adults and schools that this boy must learn while sitting still all day!

The cure is of course not Ritulin, but rather to allow the boy sufficient physical exhaustion! It is very easy. All it takes is a parent capable of respect for this natural child and for the body. This is the simple technology of applied yin and yang.

Meditation is never something you can "do" or directly teach. It has nothing to do with sitting down silently on a Tuesday night in yoga class. Meditation is a state of mind that cannot be entered by doing or intending, least of all by adopting the lotus position.

You can meditate during a game of volleyball, during sex, during a musical performance or while painting a wall. Meditation is simply to be aware of *what is*, to observe completely, like a witness.

Meditation is made of being, not doing.

The state of meditation allows us to see all there is to see, without jumping to any conclusions or attaching ourselves to preferences. Our view connects all its images to form an undivided Whole that allows us to drop the illusions arising from division. This is the supreme path to higher intelligence.

When starting out with chess we also see only those parts of the whole we give our special attention to. We are aware that our rook is under attack, or that our king has too little space to move in or that we might get to fork the two opposing rooks. These things that we have learned to spot and to recognize become important to us. But we overlook connections we are less familiar with, including our opponents' possibilities and options! We don't see the perspective of the *other*.

In meditating chess, we drop such preferences in favour of looking at the entire function on the board!

We don't look with our conditioned, subjective eyes, but with detached, neutral eyes that take it all in equally, to the most backward little pawn. We see not only where the queen seeks to go, but all the possible paths she could take to get there, including that of committing suicide.

In meditating, all intended doing comes to an end and we become the function we contemplate. Pawns are no longer wooden carvings we move about, but acquire a personality, aspirations and a position in the overall scheme of things. We can feel their potential in this life and their "will" to do their bit. We identify eventually with our pieces, until there is no player, until the player has retreated like an insightful parent who lets his kids play and do their own will. He now purely observes how the function unravels itself...

In this state no energy is wasted, no personal shortcomings influence the game and the player disappears, becomes the game...

The first time I saw this done was when Manfix had his final game in our city's senior championship when he was seventeen.

He won that last game under tremendous time pressure against the old champion, only seconds before his time fell. After which he totally ignored the huge trophy, filled with champagne and presented to him by our president. Instead of joining the celebration, he went right to discussing the game with his shattered opponent, going through all the intricacies of their shared experience and at the same time honouring the stunned man, before becoming even aware of the throng of congratulating club mates and the champagne.

I admired that. There was absolutely no pride or jubilation in Manfix, no goal-thinking, just respect for the older player, for the game itself and their interaction; and he was still enchanted by the beauty of it.

In those days I thought, like most of the other players, that Manfix looks like he is sleeping during games, and he himself wouldn't then have thought of it as meditation either.

To instinctively meditate without planning it or even knowing the word "meditate," *that* is the real thing, that thing that can lead to what they call enlightenment...

Such meditation cannot be found in a school or yoga class any easier than it can in a hurricane; it has no unique ritual or structure or definition apart from connecting the witness and the object of his observation.

I find chess uniquely suited for meditation, both to learn how to meditate and how to play chess like an artist. It invites head-centred and mentally hyperactive people to engage in an exercise that begins with where they are already and ends with getting where they need to get—out of their head!

This then becomes a permanent ability over time—but it can sometimes be achieved quite quickly:

Try "marathon chess!" The mind and its concentration eventually come to a stall after about five to seven hours of continuous thinking... So, if you play for much longer, your subconscious mind (or your dreaming!) will take over and, provided you sustain yourself with fruit sugars you eventually start meditating instead of forcing yourself to "think" any longer...

I had a marathon blitz-session once, with an equally strong player, which lasted for thirty-six hours. Crazy? Definitely! But we were both far from doing any more thinking after ten hours and lasted longer only because it cost us no further concentration- energy after that, and because we enjoyed the experience so much. It was crazy, but educational to see what is possible.

The smart way is to do such a thing only once and later recollect the feeling (as with power plants...), using only the recollection to get back into meditation quicker and quicker. But you cannot "do" it—you need to let go into it.

Don't even try teaching children meditation! The word alone kills it! Intact kids meditate naturally! While they play, while they do nothing, while adults don't interfere...

Just let them be, give them alone-time, do-nothing time, respect.

Honour their meditative states by recognizing them! A sign for their bedroom door— "Don't knock" can be an expression of such respect, and so is withholding your loud words from an entranced child.

As long as you see meditation as some Asian ritual on a yoga mat, with eyes closed and fingers touching Buddha-like on your neatly folded lotus legs on Tuesday nights, you cannot discover it in any of those many other places... It remains a particular exercise you do in order to—what? Relax?

True meditation knows no such preferences and prerequisites and cultural positions. It applies to every situation, every position, every time, all the time and everywhere! That is its very nature!

African tribal people, who have never heard the word—meditate.

The cat purring in its sunny nook—meditates.

The trees dripping in the rainforest—meditate.

Children also naturally meditate.

It is nothing special, yet nothing is more special.

The greatest virtue in the world of chess lies not in the winning or in the learning or even in its beauty as much as it can be found in eventually becoming a witness to all that and all else that *is*. An egoless servant of truth.

When you meditate chess, never suppress or try to chase away distracting thoughts! Just don't feed them your attention! Feel your purpose and the possibilities to get there! Be aware of all the functions on the board, including accidental crumbs, the clock, the table, the energy and gestures of your partner. You are aware of your spouse at home. Aware of how you feel and of who you are. And none of that interferes with any concentration since there isn't any. Chess is a part of being, as is breathing and it is just as effortless. You simply are calmly aware of it all.

Only as long as you resist the world by calling it a distraction will your creative energy attach to it as a distraction and cause a split in your reality! And if you try not to think, it will be that *try* which inevitably fills up your brain...Try not to think of a thing and it takes the foremost position in your brain! You cannot *try* not to think—that would be thinking very hard indeed!

The way to meditate is to embrace the opposites and the world that *is*, desired or feared, with quiet acceptance, like a perfect witness. How would it help to think or "do" when you're just a witness? You're too busy watching...

Thinking ponders the questions, while meditation looks at the answers that are always right in front of us, given long ago by the Gods or Nature, and still spread out for us as ageless explanations, as in a leaf or a fern-tree, by Nature and by life itself, on our chess-boards, in our children...

The tree poses many questions to the thinker, but to meditation the tree itself is the complete answer as to what there *is*. A butterfly—the complete answer as to what there *is,* and quite without a need for dissections, analyses and hypotheses.

And a chess position equally is the complete answer to what there *is*!

To learn meditation is to look into the eyes of a baby! To be open enough for actual reality.

All we then need do is *really* look!

Chapter 18: Chess for telepathy

Do you believe in telepathy? Belief doesn't really matter one bit.

Probably you have experienced two people simultaneously saying the same thing?

Or a friend you just wanted to call rang you at that same moment...?

Or maybe you know identical twins, whose identity of thought can often be baffling and not be explained by genetics alone?

This phenomenon of two or more people sharing the same thought is actually quite common. It explains the fact that many inventions are made at the same time by two or more scientists in very different parts of the world. Physics calls this "synchronicity..."

Synchronicity between people can be observed in very old couples who start and finish sentences for each other or in a team of boys, all reacting to the same ball.

An obvious example for this is an orchestra, where each player has to be on the same wave-length, with the same music and its associated emotions. Or think of a tantric couple making love, dancing to their own inner music...

And fashion also—teenagers, standing in near identical postures all over the world, holding a mobile phone while walking and speaking the alien language only they speak! Synchronicity certainly exists, but what exactly is it and what does it have to do with telepathy?

When two identical glasses are hit with a metal spoon, they will give off a sound of identical frequency. Similarly, when people are very alike and in a situation that unifies their emotional and rational dispositions, as in a lion attack, or in singing together—synchronicity can spontaneously occur.

It happens actually much of the time, as it does with animals too. When you watch a swarm of birds or fish, you will notice that it does not follow a leader. There is no reaction time between individual animals following each other. All the birds and fish turn at the exact same time as if they were *one body*!

In a rugby game or in synchronized swimming we aim to achieve just this kind of synchronicity in order to have an effective team. Synchronicity is not haphazard but can be cultivated to a very high degree, which is, after subtracting fiction and Hollywood-notions, precisely what we would call telepathy. Every All Black knows this feeling in his bones...

But what happens, when synchronicity of mind does not relate to physical movements or simple thoughts, but instead to consciousness itself? What happens, when two people sit together quietly for hours, holding nearly identical content in their minds?

For beginners at chess and for young children there are still vast differences in their individual views of the game and of reality. But the better they get, the more they will agree on a common reality! Chess-masters see the same identical reality when looking at a position! This increasing agreement on the perception of reality marks the way to insight as well as to telepathy...

When two players hold nearly identical content in their minds and meditate on this content together for hours, they achieve a particularly high state of this synchronicity!

Normally, telepathy arises from empathy (synchronicity of feeling) between people close to each other, but synchronicity of mind-content can lead to similar results.

There is no other occasion apart from chess and tantric foreplay, where two people sit quietly together for a long time, meditating together on their shared awareness!

Intense shared meditations foster the ability to perceive another person's awareness and can in fact lead to what we call telepathy. For those players interested further in how to develop useful levels of telepathy, there is a method which provides an effective exercise to that effect: chess with four players!

The rules remain unchanged. There are no pieces passed on as in "tandem chess" and everything is the same as normal, except that two players have two opponents, moving alternately. There is no talking, so the player has to guess his partner's ideas and harmonize his own plans with hers. Both partners contribute to a plan they develop together, constantly guessing at what each of them wants to do. First, they are tempted to swear at each other for sabotaging their pre-planned manoeuvres, but after a while they tend to adapt to each other's way of seeing a *common* reality.

Some people, even good players, never learn to synchronize with their partners and will deny the telepathic state. But others learn to play as if from one mind! These players will develop telepathic ability when they continue to practise this kind of double-chess. They learn to *see* each other's ideas to such a degree, that all their manoeuvres spring from one plan, which is never spoken and yet quite clear to both partners...

Sometimes, it is as if a single player makes all the moves, consistent with a single plan.

After playing double chess for a few hours, partners are often surprisingly aligned to each other and keep acting like identical twins, speaking at the same time, sneezing and ordering pizza together. They see "eye to eye."

Double chess is a wonderful family activity that allows children's and parents' minds to mingle and to cooperate when tensions and generation gaps threaten the family peace...

Just sitting together quietly as a family, playing double-chess at TV-time, does real wonders whether you believe in telepathy or not! It is even better not to "believe," just as it is better not to already "believe" in a God you still seek and have as to yet not found evidence for... What you "believe" is always somebody else's truth and a false god. In order to find your *own* truth, you need to learn seeing for yourself! And then believe what you see!

If you are aware enough to recognize the possibility and potential of higher abilities in humans—why would you deny your children such a chance at developing one of them?

Why limit our children to our horizons? Why not instead shed the arrogance of believing we already know most of what really matters?

What do you suppose it could do when you and your kid work on the same side on a shared plan for an hour, where you don't dominate, guide, instruct or even talk?

What do you think this will do at a time when you see an alien when looking at your fourteen-year old who wants to move out and thinks you a prehistoric fossil...?

Chapter 19: Love and Beauty

In a game with my oldest daughter Mana it was her turn. My next move was to give check-mate with my queen. Her pawn, about to morph into a queen, could not stop that, since she had no check.

So, I said "you're just a move too late, sweet thing" —and Mana looked at me with big eyes—converting into a knight instead! Check! "And mate in four" whispered the little assassin...

"You're such a beauty!!" I jumped and danced all over the place. It was so elegant, with just a knight and a few pawns—against my overwhelming force of heavy artillery threatening mate! So very beautiful!

And I loved my little girl so dearly for it, for finding deeper truth, for having self-belief, for unfolding her intelligence. For out-playing her God...

There are so many moments of great beauty in good games of chess! Moments, where logic and craft and reason do not suffice to explain, and where we are struck with revelation, with something that may still be of logic and of reason in hindsight, but that is now new, surprising, unexpected and beautiful in its elegant manifestation.

It fills the heart when it is thus heaved up like new-found treasure, or pulled up like an exotic fish that will feed the entire family with its flesh and its colors...

Although the board and pieces still look unchanged to the uninitiated, there is suddenly immense beauty on the board that those with eyes to see can behold and recognize. Wherein lies this beauty, one may well ask and what is beauty beyond a subjective feeling?

Well, in the case of Mana's super-move the beauty lay in discovering a deeper truth that would change all of reality. A truth even I hadn't seen.

The discovery of truth seems to generally lie at the heart of what we see as beautiful.

The famous, "golden" proportion of 0.618 for example is a deep mathematical truth which we become aware of when looking at a face cast in this same proportion. Models have facial proportions of very close to 0.618 and that is why we find them pretty. It is like that with all art-work, painting and with music, where what we experience as beautiful is simply a mathematically defined truth revealing itself.

It is very beautiful to all sane people to simply look at the natural world. Why? Because Nature holds and reveals the deepest truths of all and is utterly mathematical, logical, purposeful and wise in its symbolism when doing so! Nature knows the divine, the deepest truths, and this is why we experience it as beautiful.

Being touched by a lover who fully understands who we really are, is thus beautiful.

To me beauty lies in watching (my) children and to see them growing out of the box, away from cultural dogma, and towards their own free, self-discovered awareness of Self and of realty. To see them fathoming their humanity and the purpose of their lives is what I experience as beauty, and this is also what defines my deepest, purest love.

What is love? A thousand things to a thousand people, certainly. Anything objective? Apart from the illusions of romantic and possessive love, or those of parental and possessive love?

Those feelings we commonly call "love," because they make us all feel "good" and cozy and protected and desired and worthy—those are not actual love, if love is to be more than the satisfaction of selfish need! But they are all most of us know...

No, real love is not a feeling. It is a power, a force, and it only happens on the other side of self-interest! This is true for both lovers and parents. Your best chance to find this very rare thing lies probably in watching a hobby gardener, or a few enlightened parents, the odd dog and remote tribal elders...

Forget Mother Theresa, Christian donors to charities, and all those who want to earn themselves a "heaven" or a do-gooder's righteous feeling! Selfishness and self-promotion is commonly what you find at the bottom of their motivations...

Love and beauty are more than feelings or social agreements. They arise from doing things as they are *supposed* to be done. Supposed by the heart, by intuition, the senses, supposed by Nature! And in being that which you are, without asking for reward.

When looking at your child, you need to let go of all the distorting images pertaining to what you fear or like to see. You need to let go of the idea of your child as an unfinished adult, as owned by you and of thinking you always know best.

Instead look and see what there already is!

Look at your child, not as something you made, but as a respected visitor!

Without a doubt, it can be extremely painful to thus strip off all your selfish motives and to drop the parental "authority" to shape a child in your image. But love, real love, can *only* be found on this path of surrender, of giving up control, of respecting the other.

Torn and shredded by those growing-pains of parental becoming as we parents all are, it is this path of surrender which by every small step reveals true beauty in ourselves, in our child and in all with eyes to see...

Some call that love.

Chapter 20: Duality and Oneness

Why do Zen-masters ask their students to listen to "one hand clapping" or to a "soundless sound?" Why do they consider paradoxical opposites to be the most direct path to Oneness and to enlightenment?

This question is identical to the one asking why the yin/yang symbol is made of two equal and opposite forces, forming a whole—or why there is parent and child.

Our world appears to be split into such polarities throughout: There is an anti-quark to every quark, a positron for every electron, a left with every right, up and down, good and bad, warm and cold, inside and outside. Everything comes in pairs of symmetric dualities, a yin and a yang to all things. This is why things can only be fully understood in terms of their polarity, their symmetry, which defines the spectrum of their reality.

Humans can only be understood by understanding man and woman equally. If you are a man, you don't understand what it means to be human until you get to really know a woman. And if you are old, you will find wisdom mostly in understanding children!

Growing into adults, we must overcome but not lose our inner child to remain undivided...

On a spiritual level, we can only see the light if we first face darkness and if we unify those opposites of what we suppose we are.

It is not enough to decide for "good" and against "bad," because this either/or-decision leads into a further split of consciousness and into narrow places, like "good kids" and "bad kids," and "us and them, black and white. "Good" will thus always be us, and "bad" will only be the others. In any conflict with our kids—it is then always *their* fault...

Only if we understand the Oneness behind good/bad, which is ethical consideration, will we be free enough to make ethical choices.

To decide for left or right leads us into arbitrary or pre-ordained, divisive and limited directions. These things are unfortunately never considered in child education.

Left is nothing without right, just as only the left hand clapping produces no sound. Left does not even exist theoretically independently from right, as there is never any yin without a corresponding yang.

So, what should we do, as practical people, when we come to a crossroad with the signs "Left" and "Right?" Most people make an automatic either/or decision here, even if it is utterly arbitrary! They lean to the left or are always right...

Henry Miller once said "if you come to a fork in the road—take it!" And this alone is the enlightened view! Just because there are only two options on offer—left and right, that does not, to the intelligent, take away the options of going back, sitting down, burying a hole or to jump like a kangaroo across the paddock between the two opposite roads!

The enlightened view is to never get trapped by either/or decisions, but to avail oneself of all the options as a free agent. That is the path from duality to Oneness, from mental slavery to freedom and to exceptional parenting!

"Can I go to that party?" To just say "no!" to such a question leads to division, confrontation and role-assertion! You have created a battle-field! Why not hear about the party and the who, where, and why of it, and come to a mutual decision? If you still disagree, why not negotiate a deal?

Whether dualities trap us into illusions of being "good" or "right," "down" or "up there," depends on whether we buy into the notion of deciding for one or the other. Taking the "right" road divides the available freedom into two fragmented pieces every time, it creates a "wrong" road and ignores all the other freedoms, like climbing a tree or building a tunnel. It narrows us down!

It makes us believe that our kids need us to constantly correct them if they are to learn doing anything the "right," that is our own, way.

In the long run, either/or decisions form a habit of splitting the world as we should know it and then discard half of it... In the individual, we call this a split or schizoid personality! When it becomes fearfully disorienting, we call it schizophrenia. When a whole culture is based on it, we see it as normal...

This is why the Taoist masters suggest the other way—to bring the opposites together, to see their underlying Oneness. "Listen to the sound of silence" keeps us listening, while avoiding all the particular and dividing sounds that scatter our consciousness into fragmentation.

What those masters do is what I call "chess-parenting!" It does not divide the world but brings imagined opposites together into one. Parenting in this understanding is a two-way street.

As a society, we have utterly subscribed to an either/or- philosophy where opposites totally exclude each other. We are good and the others are bad...

If we are on the "right" in politics, we see no merit in socialist thought. If we are a woman, we cannot understand men. If we are Israelis, we cannot feel for suffering Palestinian children. We belong to a group, and people outside this group—are the "others..."

And we don't like "others" like "niggers," "chinks," "punks," "prostitutes," "gang-members," or anybody who is different from the normal, because we relate only to our own side of a world we ourselves have divided. We are the master-fools of a divided world...

The "other side" is dark, different, most often "bad" and eventually— "evil!"

This obsession to divide and to thus create this "evil" is the root cause of war, sexism, racism, terrorism, of ineffective politics, poor parenting and personal ignorance.

It is the actual "original sin" and it is the essence of what we teach our children...

There is of course nothing wrong with duality as such, which is the Janus-face of Oneness—step two after the first step of Creation.

Light and darkness complement each other and are as "good" as each other!

The problems start when we put light above darkness, thinking it superior!

And that is what we always do!

We associate the dark with the devil and with fear and ignorance, while celebrating the light as divine and enlightening. And BANG—we have split the world! We see none of its colours now; we become blinded by too much light and are afraid of the dark. As chess-players we believe that playing the white stones is an advantage...

As parents, we are "always right," always in the superior, commanding parent-role, which leaves our kids, the over-controlled receivers of our proclaimed wisdom, to be regulated into conformity by our moral dogmas and cultural expectations. If we are religious, we even represent the word of God and see our kids as tainted by original sin and in need to be saved by conforming to our views...

Without this splitting-off from the actual Oneness there could never be a war, or any violence, or mental illness and there would be no rebellious teenager!

Our only chance to heal this fundamental rift between opposites, which splinters out to be also a rift between mind and body, thinking and emotion, and between family members, is to make decisive use of those factors in life that still have unifying character!

The two best existing possibilities for this purpose are, obvious to the sober observer—sex and love. They are nature's own ultimate devices to keep the balance between fragmented isolation and unifying Oneness.

In sex and love we can completely overcome isolation and fragmentation and thus experience temporary Oneness in profound plateau-orgasms and in blissful surrender of our monstrous western ego.

But unfortunately, we do not know how to *really* love or how to have great sex! Love has become a word for sex or for infatuation, or for some good feeling we get when feeling wanted. It has little to do with selflessness or devotion or unconditional giving. We want to receive at least as much as we give...

Love is thus no longer a unifying force! As consumers, we know only possessive love, jealous love, romantic infatuation, biological need and calculated deals. There is no unifying power in any of that, only further division.

The art of sexual loving is equally a lost and forgotten one... Sex is a race towards orgasm which may last for half an hour (the race that is) —a frantic "doing" to receive quick gratification. To both men and women sex is only a tiny fraction of what it could be and it fails to effectively bring them together emotionally or energetically.

As a consequence of this inability to reconnect, a huge black hole has opened up on the side of unifying thought in our time! Science is now entirely about fragmentation, as in analysis of compounds, atoms and concepts, and about specialization to a point where no scientist looks beyond the narrow scope of his field any more—so blindly specialized is he.

We can split the atom but not put it back together!

As parents, we look at our children not as they are, but at how they measure up to our expectations! We weigh them with our scales, measure them with our yard-sticks, calculate their calories and feed them our concepts...

How can we still, if only as individuals, get away from this duality-trap and find completeness? Oneness? Enlightened parenting? Undisturbed children?

The answer to this is that you can never get away from traps or from duality. Trying to escape from duality cannot work. The only thing that works is to balance and master duality to a point where Oneness reveals itself! So instead of running from it, do what the masters recommend—meditate on paradox! You choose clearly polarised duality concepts and practise them, meditate them. When your kids raise their voices, listen to the soundless sound before you speak!

Consider that your child's view of the world has merit equal to yours!

Consider that your child too is helping you to grow up!

Consider how crazy *you* must appear to your teen!

Chess is the ultimate polar duality concept wrapped in a game! It is an interactive window to a supposedly separate reality, a parallel and highly symbolic universe, a mirror for real life. As black and white, two players compete against each other for supremacy in utmost polarity. The outcome is either winning or losing or being undecided in a battle between the forces of light and dark...

The beginner is totally caught up in this polar structure, identifies with the colour he plays and with his side of the table. He either wins or loses, in chess as in argument! His "plans" are only for his own pieces and he sees only the parent's point of view.

If he plays white, he sees the white position as *his* and as more important than the position for black! He is only half responsible! He wonders what the other side might do, but he is not responsible for that half of reality... He is white and concentrates on his own moves only—like the preaching parent!

If, however, a player is to advance to the level of true understanding, this identification with *his* side of the board needs to be dropped! He then realizes that the moves for black have to be considered just as much as the white moves! We may not know what our opponent will play, but we need to consider what he *could* play, which is his best move. It does not matter at all what colour the pieces are and who they belong to. The whole game is a single function that each player owns in its entirety, while he considers both sides equally in order to understand it at all!

At this stage, the importance of colour and of which side a player belongs to, ceases to exist. He now looks at the whole function as if he were playing both sides or against himself. As if he'd care for both Israelis *and* Palestinians! As if he saw the world through his teenager's eyes, as well!

When this happens, duality is transcended into Oneness! There is now no opponent. There is only a partner who intimately shares our consciousness of the two polar sides of a shared reality!

It is vital to recognize duality as the final step before reaching Oneness, not purely its antithesis or a mere hindrance.

We need not despise the body when we cultivate the soul! We need not "fight evil" to know good! We need not control and suppress our kids' natural impulses to teach them "discipline!" We only need to bring the opposites together to get over our dividing world view.

It is the ultimate illusion to think of opposites as excluding each other. Reality is not like that! There is no devil to balance god! There is only the divine and ignorance thereof! We only need a devil because we are trapped by duality, avoiding Oneness and real freedom—even in our Gods.

Once we see the entire function on a chess board, we could play with two sets of white pieces, since colour is no longer relevant. It is the same with racism—once we see the entire human being, colour becomes irrelevant, one in a billion details.

Chess exercises this ability to transcend duality, and it leaves us no chance to fool ourselves into believing ourselves more advanced than we really are! It also keeps any unnecessary mysticism out of self-development and it has no cultural, dogmatic, undesirable or arbitrary notions of any kind.

So, you can either play on half a board with only your white pieces—or you can look at both sides of the truth with equal interest!

There is then no need to even own chess pieces because you can just visualize them. You can close your eyes, lie in a hammock and play chess blind—seeing it all.

You are then aware of your child as having her own path in life!

When you don't need a board or pieces or an opponent in order to have a good game, you have transcended duality. You have nothing and therefore everything.

You do nothing and yet you have completed the work.

You can hear the soundless sound.

From here on you can be a parent who no longer gets trapped into confrontational role games based on the "generation gap", falling no longer for the usual authority and control issues. You have real power—and so do your children!

No longer do you always know better, telling your kids what to do and think. Now you can listen to the things your kids know, admire what they do, learn from it. And if you tell your story well and without condescension, they will listen to you too!

Such a parent does not believe himself to be the "head" of a family, just because he brings home the bacon. He respects his child's contributions, which may be house-work or a good idea, or a developing attitude—as equal contribution.

The undivided parent does not disrespect his toddler or make her the recipient of untrue stories about Easter-rabbits, Santa Clauses, baby-Jesuses and goat-footed devils.

He is an unaffected guide and well-respected elder—not the representative of his culture and religion who indoctrinates his mini-me to embrace his own and his culture's version of reality.

A respectful parent does not teach Christianity or Islam or join his kid to the Jehovah's witnesses! This is arrogantly disrespectful and possessive programming and child abuse—not parenting!

A parent only points out the various possible views, lets the child compare their human appeal, and allows her to put it aside after that.

He then proceeds to live examples the child can admire and learn from! He shows self-responsibility and cultivates self-respect and self-discipline and is showing actual respect and courtesy to other lifeforms. He realizes that true competence, rather than praise, leads to self-acceptance and that competence grows not from doing what you are told to do, but from looking at all things from all sides, in your own way, and then making well-weighed responsible choices.

A child will never need to rebel against a truly respectful parent, because his authority is natural, not imposed, and his "rules" easily accepted, helpful, and not limiting.

The chess-parent is not stuck in a parent-role! He is sometimes just a friend, at times a task-master, and when he has a tooth-ache, he gets mothered by his little girl. His relationships are based on equality and mutual respect.

The duality of constantly fighting parents and the war between generations are not in the "nature of things," as we tend to believe, or it would exist in every society! It is self-created!

In natural societies, there is usually no reality-split at all, nor do boys or girls often argue or fight! Instead of following fancy educational theories they simply have Oneness in their family, based on mutual respect, trust and the feeling of sitting in the same boat.

The chess-parent is not the all-knowing king of his family. He is a tiger for and not towards his children! He can always be questioned. He does not need to ask for obedience, because he has the respect and love of his family.

He may not even need a TV set, because he has things to offer that his kids prefer!

The strategic parent needs very little tactical guile in raising his kids. His strategy is to sort himself out and respect his own self early on. To "grow up" alongside his kids in a balanced, mutual partnership!

He does not have "custody" of his children, but rather of himself!

He gets over his own divisions, his black-and-white cultural views and trusts the kids will follow his and others' example where it is strong and worth following. They usually do.

Other books by Fritz Blackburn:

- Travel-parenting: https://books2read.com/u/mlGEYM

- Reality and Shit: https://books2read.com/u/3kweBR

- The Cosmic Egg: https://books2read.com/u/mqaGO9

About the Author

Fritz Blackburn, born in Augsburg, Germany, studied law and economics before he traveled the world on a shoe-string and lived in remote cultures. He learned about mind development from Mexican shamans like Maria Sabina and explored techniques that cultivate the human potential. He taught yoga in the Philippines where he ran his own school on Boracay Island. He settled in New Zealand, worked as a holistic healer and continued travel with his two daughters.